THE FACE OF MARYLAND

STATE HOUSE, ST. MARYS CITY

THE FACE OF MARYLAND

A. AUBREY BODINE

Honorary Fellow of the Photographic Society of America
Fellow of the National Press Photographers

Published by Bodine and Associates, Inc., Baltimore

CHARLES CENTER AT NIGHT, FROM JACOB FRANCE FOUNTAIN

Library of Congress Catalog No. 79-133333
Standard Book Number 910254-30-3
Printed in the United States of America
Copyright 1970, Bodine & Associates, Inc.

THIRD EDITION

FOREWORD

Someone once said, "Genius is the infinite capacity for taking pains." A. Aubrey Bodine, in addition to rare talent, has that capacity. To get sunlight, mist or shadow precisely the way he wants them, this most patient man will wait hours; go back, even great distances; and, if necessary, postpone taking the picture for months. It is not uncommon to hear him say, "Let's wait until the middle of April"—this may be February—"then the sun will be on its right axis for that shot." (All this can be disconcerting to the editor who needs a picture in a hurry. Once when asked how an assignment turned out, Bodine replied, "Didn't open my camera. I'm having them dig a pit so I can get silhouettes from a new angle.") When he thinks a traffic sign detracts from a scene he is photographing, he covers it with a sign of his own design. He prevails upon businessmen and government officials, even the Governor, to have branches trimmed, signs, poles and sometimes outbuildings moved if they obstruct his best camera angle. The one-way arrow on Tyson Street (Page 22) is hidden by a Bodine sign. The picture of the Brice House (Page 108) could be made from this angle only after an obstruction was removed. He takes as much time and trouble in his darkroom as he does with his camera. He does all his own developing and printing, and will spend hours if necessary to make a print just the way he wants it. He has developed darkroom techniques that even skilled photographers admit they cannot duplicate.

Contrary to what many think, Bodine does not achieve his results with a lot of expensive equipment. Many of the pictures in this book were made with a 5 by 7-inch view camera so battered and worn that it looks as if it might have been abandoned on a battlefield by Mathew Brady. Not one for gadgets, Bodine's basic accessories are a wooden tripod, a black cloth, a few filters, a compass, a machete to cut away brush that gets in the way of a view, and a bee smoker to provide wisps of smoke.

To see what he could do without even that equipment he has been sent out with only a box camera. The results were typical of his work. The reason, of course, is that the essence of the Bodine photograph is the man himself. He is an artist by instinct and training, with an unerring sense of proportion and composition. He has a deep appreciation of beauty in all its forms and moods. Heart and mind create the photograph that is distinguished by its beauty, clarity and air of tranquility. In looking at one of his pictures I am usually struck first by its beauty, then by its simplicity of form. I think that what he leaves out of a picture is almost as important as what he allows into it. He has a gift for isolating and dramatizing beauty, and of hiding or subduing anything that detracts from it. If I come upon a view that I have first seen in a Bodine picture, I am often disappointed. Actuality is seldom as beautiful as Bodine's portrayal. An example of what he can do appears on page 25. The Administration Building of the Johns Hopkins Hospital has character, but certainly not the grace and beauty Bodine achieves.

Though most of his work has been made for *The Sun Magazine*, it is more than newspaper photography. His prints have won awards in all parts of the world. They hang in museums, in libraries and in the Smithsonian Institution, where fourteen are on permanent exhibition. Clipped from the *Magazine*, the pictures are used in schools, treasured in scrapbooks, and tacked up in crossroad garages. They have a universal and continuing appeal.

I believe that Bodine's photographs will be meaningful to those who follow us because they are made by a man who knows and loves his native land, and who has the talent and capacity to blend love and knowledge with chemicals and magic to create images of lasting value.

Harold A. Williams

WASHINGTON PLACE, FLOWER MART DAY—1956

The Face of Maryland

MY MAIN JOB as photographic director of *The Sun Magazine* is to take pictures of Maryland and its people. I think it is one of the most rewarding jobs there are. I travel to all parts of the State—a State that has everything from ocean to mountains—and meet all sorts of interesting people—watermen, mountaineers, antiquarians, strip miners, scientists and the Amish of St. Marys County. In the course of my picture taking I often pick up unusual facts that give more meaning to the photographs. I would like to tell you about some of these things, and, here and there, add some personal comment.

The picture on page 85 was made on Deils Island, Deal Island, or Deals Island—take your choice. One of Maryland's great cartographers, Simon Martinet, chose Deils, the Post Office Department selected Deal. I prefer Deals, and so do most of the natives. The view through the pound net was made at the packing house of my friend Richard Webster. The two skipjacks are the *Sigsbee* and *Upshur Q.*

The Enoch Pratt Free Library (Page 14) is one of the most efficient institutions in Baltimore and it seldom makes a mistake. But my camera recorded one of its rare errors. The Maryland flag is flying upside down.

For certain pictures I prefer infra-red film; I used it for the State Office Building (Page 20), the office buildings on page 17 and the Church Spires in Frederick (126). I felt the stark style of the State Office Building was an invitation to put emphasis on the vertical lines, hence the use of infra-red here. Incidentally I felt automobiles in the foreground of this picture would spoil the view so I waited until the Fourth of July to make my picture. The shot of the Commercial Credit and Chesapeake & Potomac Telephone Company buildings was made with a wide angle lens of 135 degrees. I like this view of the buildings because it dramatizes the commercial growth and importance of Baltimore.

I like to wander through old cemeteries, particularly Green Mount because it has such unusual grave markers, including an upside down bathtub. This picture of Green Mount (Page 23) won a national award. I used the prize money to help buy one of the few remaining lots in the old section where any type of marker is acceptable. If I want to put an iron tripod and camera on my lot I may.

I have never enjoyed watching the construction of anything as much as I did that of the Cathedral of Mary Our Queen (Page 36). I think I was awed by the realization that nothing so fine and so elaborate would be done again in Baltimore, in my lifetime, at least. During the two years of building I made many pictures. These were used in a special issue of our *Magazine*. Some also appeared in a handsome guide book of the cathedral which was written by the Rev. J. Joseph Gallagher. Archbishop Francis P. Keough presented me with a specially bound copy of the guide which was inscribed by him, "To A. Aubrey Bodine. With gratitude and appreciation for his kindness and artistry."

Another favorite building of mine is the Maryland Institute (Page 50). I studied design here, and I will always be grateful for the help I received from a dedicated faculty. The tuition I paid the Institute was the best investment I ever made.

If I were asked to select the most interesting and scenic county of the Eastern Shore, I would, without hesitation, pick Dorchester (Pages 70 and 71). It has hundreds of miles of interesting shoreline along rivers, creeks, bays and coves. One of the most picturesque spots in the county is Hoopers Island, a crabbing and fishing center. During the height of the crab season, housewives who do crab-picking as part-time work, are summoned to the packing houses from their homes by the toot of a whistle.

Ask a waterman (Page 86) how things are going and he will usually reply, "Had a slim day." But I have noticed that watermen who work regularly can make a comfortable living. Most of them own their own boats, homes and cars. And, above all, they are supremely independent, and I cannot help but envy this independence and their way of life.

There are not many haul seiners, but they surely are the most abused group of watermen on the Bay. Sport and commercial fishermen blame them whenever fishing gets bad. I personally think this is a lot of nonsense. I spent a day traveling with some haul seiners from Rock Hall, who included three generations in the picture on page 90. They fished much the way their ancestors fished and at the end of a hard day's work they had landed about five dollars worth of marketable fish. At lunch time the boats were beached and biscuits and fish were prepared on an old grill. It was a wonderful lunch.

The Brice House (Page 108) is one of Maryland's most majestic houses. The two main chimneys contain enough brick to build one or two modern ranch-type homes. Few Marylanders realize that Annapolis contains more original Colonial and Georgian homes than any other city in America. Still standing and in a good state of preservation are the homes of three Signers of the Declaration of Independence—Samuel Chase, Charles Carroll of Carrollton and William Paca.

Many years ago Mark Watson, at that time editor of *The Sunday Sun,* sent me to Charles County to make pictures of the ruins of Governor William Smallwood's home (Page 119). After much searching, and with the help of a local historian, I found, in a deep tangle of bushes, some brick walls. Now, after painstaking research and careful building under the direction of my friend Henry Powell Hopkins, the Smallwood house has been rebuilt. Baltimore and Maryland have a number of priceless buildings that need saving. Why do people wait until these places are in ruins before something is done?

I regard Tulip Hill (Page 121) as one of Maryland's great houses. It has one of the loveliest of settings, surrounded by majestic trees. Its interior and furnishings are something to behold. H. Chandlee Forman, an authority on old Maryland and Virginia houses, once told me that he considers the canopy over the doorway to be the finest he has ever seen. One personal note: I am an inveterate corncob pipe smoker, and I use more matches than tobacco. When I am at Tulip Hill—which I regard as a perfect house and exquisitely kept—I put my matches in my pocket and risk burning my coat rather than soil one of its ashtrays.

Frederick is, by far, the loveliest town in Maryland. Some of its side streets, lined with ancient one and two-story brick houses, are absolute gems. On some of these streets one can still find log cabins that have been hidden behind clapboard. The spires of Frederick (Page 126) were photographed from the Baker Carillon with a telephoto lens and infra-red film.

I think the stone fences of Frederick and Washington counties (Page 128) are perfectly beautiful. Many are made from limestone and natives often refer to them as "lime fences." The stones are skillfully stacked without cement. I have heard stonemasons marvel at the craftsmanship in these fences, some of which have been standing for over 200 years.

Every fall for many years I have roamed the Maryland countryside searching for rolling fields filled with corn shocks. With the right light and angle one can't help but get a beautiful picture. The scene pictured on page 138 might be one of the last such shots I will ever make. It takes about twenty acres of corn shocks to make a good picture. These days farmers are reluctant to shock that much corn because of the hand labor involved. Most large farms now use mechanical cornhuskers and because of these machines the corn is no longer shocked.

Burnside Bridge (Page 152) has long been a favorite subject. One cannot help but marvel at the skilled handiwork that built such bridges. This one cost but $2,300—less than the cost of the car I drive or the camera equipment I carry in the trunk. This picture was made early on an April morning so that the mist would create a dramatic feeling.

A. AUBREY BODINE, Hon. F.P.S.A., F.N.P.P.
Baltimore, Maryland, September, 1970

"In the Darkroom" by Stanislav Rembski

THE BALTIMORE SKYLINE FROM FEDERAL HILL—1970

Baltimore

BALTIMORE at daybreak, when the sun splashes across the eastern face of the city . . . Baltimore at sunset, in repose and in silhouette . . . Baltimore in the freshness of a Maryland spring . . . on a summer afternoon . . . and under a winter's snow, quiet and serene.

Fort McHenry . . . the Johns Hopkins Hospital . . . the Pratt Library . . . the Walters Art Gallery . . . Peabody . . . beautiful and urbane Mount Vernon Place . . . the old Baltimore of Hollins Market, near which H. L. Mencken lived, with its open stalls under canvas . . . the new Baltimore of Friendship's jet airport and shining, modern buildings—the vast Social Security headquarters, and the complex of State office buildings . . . the great port with 40 miles of waterfront, the most exciting and romantic part of Baltimore . . . home of the world's largest steel mill . . . and its largest spice factory . . . city of churches . . . city of schools . . . Baltimore, famous for its oyster roasts . . . Baltimore, famous for the Preakness, the Colts, the Orioles, the Maryland Hunt Cup . . . lacrosse center of the nation . . . Baltimore, many things to many people . . . This is the city that A. Aubrey Bodine has pictured.

BATTLE MONUMENT . . . A tribute to the men who fell at North Point and Fort McHenry in the War of 1812, this is the third-oldest of the many memorials in Baltimore, "the Monumental City." It was designed by the noted Maximilian Godefroy, and its cornerstone was laid in 1815. It is pictured on the City Seal and on the City Flag.

CITY HALL . . . The cornerstone was laid for Baltimore City Hall in 1867 and the Renaissance-style structure was dedicated in 1875. The height from the basement floor to the top of the cast iron dome is 236 feet. The building covers an area of 35,462 square feet, and is viewed here across City Hall Plaza. Visible on the skyline just to the left of the dome is part of the Blaustein Building; to the right of the dome is the top of the Arlington Federal Building.

THE PEABODY . . . The Peabody Institute and Conservatory of Music is world famous. It was endowed by George Peabody, one of Baltimore's great benefactors, and ground was broken in 1859. Behind these buildings are modern dormitories designed by Edward Durrell Stone.

THE JACOBS MANSION . . . The largest and most elaborate town house in Baltimore, the 40-room mansion above overlooks Mount Vernon Place and now is owned by the Engineers Club of Baltimore. An estimated $6,000,-000 was spent building, decorating and furnishing this mansion, which was designed by Stanford White. Financier Robert Garrett had the first portion built in 1884. Dr. Henry Jacobs added to it in 1905.

THOMAS-JENCKS-GLADDING . . . Built in 1851 for Dr. John Thomas and acquired 40 years later by the Jencks family, this 22-room mansion on Mount Vernon Place is considered by some to be one of the best surviving town houses in the country. The house was bought by Baltimore City in 1953 and sold ten years later to Harry Lee Gladding, who resides there after supervising an extensive restoration. The fence in foreground circles Washington Monument.

WASHINGTON MONUMENT . . . Baltimore's was the first monument to Washington begun anywhere, though not the first completed. It was begun in 1815 and finished in 1829—two years after one had been built near Boonsboro, Md. Its designer was Robert Mills. The original plan was to place the 220-foot shaft where Battle Monument now stands; that was then the center of population. But property owners there were afraid to have a shaft so tall near their homes. The remote site that has become Mount Vernon Place was donated by Col. John Eager Howard. This monument is the city's second-oldest, antedated only by a private one of 1792 honoring Columbus.

WALTERS ART GALLERY . . . Henry Walters in 1931 bequeathed to the city the building above and its collection of ancient to 19th Century art, which he and his father, William T. Walters, had made. The collection is ranked as one of America's greatest.

PRATT LIBRARY . . . More than four million books a year are circulated by the public library system that the merchant Enoch Pratt launched in 1886. The present central building, left, dates to 1933. It is noted for its functional design, open stacks, window displays.

PEABODY LIBRARY . . . Founded by banker George Peabody, but administered since 1966 by Pratt Library, this repository has books and manuscripts valued at more than $9,000,-000. In front of the spectacular central stack is the late author, John Dos Passos.

15

SHOT TOWER . . . Built in 1828, this Baltimore landmark was used for making shot. Molten lead was dropped from the top of the 234-foot tower and hardened into pellets upon hitting water at the bottom. The walls of the tower are more than five and a half feet thick at the base.

CARROLL MANSION . . . This Baltimore house was built about 1812, and in 1818 Charles Carroll, the last surviving signer of the Declaration of Independence, bought it for his daughter Mary and her husband Richard Caton. General Lafayette was entertained in the house. Carroll died in it in 1832. Restored at a cost of about $300,000 in 1967, the house is administered by Peale Museum and is open to the public on a limited basis.

STUDY IN CONTRAST . . . Graceful steps in Preston Gardens stand out against a backdrop of modern buildings that typify the revitalization of Baltimore beyond Charles Center. The buildings are 222 Saint Paul apartments, left, the Commercial Credit Building, center, and the Chesapeake and Potomac Telephone Company Building.

THE NEW BALTIMORE . . . Charles Center has given a fresh, modern look to the Baltimore skyline, with the emphasis on new buildings. Looking across Hopkins Plaza, above, from the terrace of the Federal Office Building, the Morris Mechanic Theater is just behind the lamp standard. The modern Blaustein Building is the highest structure just to the left of the standard, while the 12-story Sun Life Building is the one with the black facade. Center Plaza, below, is still another facet of the bright new face of Baltimore. This plaza is just behind One Charles Center, and the hub is wired so a Christmas tree may be displayed. Within the plaza there also is a 33-foot bronze sculpture by Francesco Somaini. The shaft was commissioned by the Baltimore Gas and Electric Company.

SIGNS OF GROWTH . . . The 17-story Federal Office Building, top left, is an $18,000,000 addition to Charles Center. Its narrow, slit-like windows remind some of a giant computer punch card. Reaching skyward, top right, are the twin tower apartments at Two Charles Center. Modernistic lamps like the one in this picture were designed by a Baltimorean and cost $7,500 each.

MERCANTILE BUILDING . . . Still other structures adding sweep and beauty to the 33-acre Charles Center area are the clean-lined Mercantile Building, left foreground, the Baltimore Hilton Hotel, on the right of the Mercantile structure, and the Baltimore Gas and Electric Company annex. Below, children watch the Jacob France memorial fountain bubble soothingly on a summer day.

SOCIAL SECURITY BUILDING . . . The vast structure, above, which stands on a 140-acre tract at Woodlawn, is Social Security headquarters for the nation. It was first occupied in 1960 and houses more than 12,000 persons in a sprawling complex with approximately 16,000,000 square feet of floor space. The ten-story section is the administration building.

STATE OFFICE BUILDING . . . Previously scattered about both Baltimore and Annapolis, in 1959 most of Maryland's State agencies were brought together under one roof—that of the fifteen-story edifice below, in Mount Royal Plaza. Separate buildings there house the State Roads Commission and the Department of Employment Security. Part of the Roads building is seen at left.

PROFESSIONAL CAMPUS . . . The University of Maryland, Baltimore campus, is a complex of six professional schools and a hospital in an area of 16 square blocks—and it is ever expanding. Some 2,500 students attend the Schools of Dentistry, Law, Medicine, Nursing, Pharmacy and Social Work. On the skyline is the University of Maryland Hospital. In the right foreground is the modern law school.

SINAI HOSPITAL . . . The imposing structure below is the principal one of ten that comprise Sinai Hospital's modern center of medical care, research and nurses' training. The hospital, which is more than a century old, moved into new buildings on a 50-acre site near the northwestern edge of town in 1953. Sinai has more than 550 physicians, beds for 480 adult patients and more than 90 bassinets. It has an annual budget of $15,000,000.

MENCKEN HOUSE . . . The three-story row house, above, at 1524 Hollins Street, was the home of Henry L. Mencken. It was here he edited the *American Mercury* and wrote "The American Language," and it was here he spent many satisfying years. The Mencken house was a house of guns and seidels, brass and cigars, but it also was a house of books. It contained a library of more than 2,000 volumes, even after tons of literary material were removed to start a Mencken Collection at Pratt Library in the 1940's. After Mencken's death in 1956, his brother August kept H. L.'s possessions, including his desk, just as he left them. August died in 1967 and the house now belongs to the University of Maryland. The Center for the Study of Voluntarism is on the first floor. A middle room is a memorial to Mr. Mencken. Upper floors have apartments for University of Maryland students.

TYSON STREET . . . The 900 block of this narrow street of tiny houses is a showplace on the edge of downtown Baltimore. Artists began to settle there in 1946, and they restored the old buildings and painted them such hues as pink, green and yellow. Professional people replaced some of the artists, but the colors remain.

BIRTHPLACE OF A KING . . . The king was the Home Run King—George Herman Ruth—one of the most beloved stars of baseball, whose record of 714 home runs still stands. The house in which he was born, at 216 Emory Street, has been restored along with adjoining ones as a shrine to one of the true all-time greats of baseball.

HOLLINS MARKET . . . Dating from 1836 and once the city's largest market of its kind, this collection of colorful outdoor stalls used to extend three blocks. Now there are perhaps a dozen stalls, covering half a block. Market days are Friday and Saturday. Despite the market's decline, some of the customers are second and third generation.

GREEN MOUNT . . . Johns Hopkins, Betsy Patterson, Enoch Pratt, Sidney Lanier and Confederate Generals William H. Winder and Joseph E. Johnston are among the dead who repose in this cemetery, the name of which is often incorrectly written as a single word. The brownstone chapel is of a Gothic design that has been praised as remarkably pure and graceful.

23

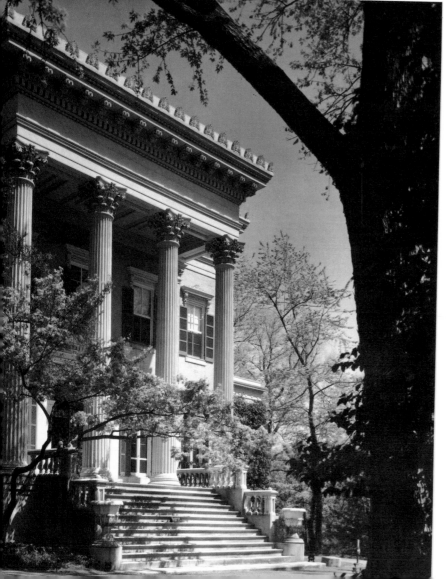

GATEWAY TO KNOWLEDGE . . . This is the Charles Street entrance to Johns Hopkins University, one of the more renowned universities in the world. It has an enrollment exceeding 10,000, including students in evening courses, and some of the finest instruction of its type is offered in its medical institutions and school of advanced international studies. The building in the center is a modern library that was dedicated in 1964.

EVERGREEN HOUSE . . . A classical revival structure built in the 1850's, this formerly was the home of John Work Garrett, a diplomat and bibliophile. He bequeathed it to the Johns Hopkins University, and it now serves as a scholars' library, museum and setting for concerts, lectures and operas.

JOHNS HOPKINS HOSPITAL . . . One of the foremost medical and research centers of the world, this 1,200-bed hospital, with its associated School of Medicine, School of Hygiene and Public Health and Welch Medical Library, draws patients and students from almost every land. It was founded in 1889 by the merchant whose name it bears. Today, tall and modern ancillary buildings surround the domed building that has long been a landmark yet now is but a small part of the complex.

SHRIVER HALL . . . A lecture hall at Johns Hopkins University, this was erected with a bequest of Alfred Jenkins Shriver, a bachelor philanthropist who died in 1939 at the age of 72. He had stipulated that its decorations include a mural portraying ten women he chose as "Famous Beauties of Baltimore." The painting is the one above.

MARYLAND INSTITUTE BRANCH . . . The Baltimore and Ohio Railroad closed Mount Royal station in 1961, but three years later the Maryland Institute bought the landmark with the imposing clocktower and spent $500,000 converting it into a branch that includes classrooms, a sculptors' studio, painting lofts and a gallery. In the background is Sutton Place apartment house.

MARYLAND HISTORICAL SOCIETY . . . Founded in 1844, the society has a priceless collection of books, manuscripts, furniture and paintings depicting Maryland's past. The wing at right is the Thomas and Hugg Memorial Building, which was completed in 1967. Money for the wing came from William S. Thomas and John L. Thomas, brothers who bequeathed $2,600,000 to the society.

DAVIDGE HALL . . . Modeled after the Pantheon, it is the original University of Maryland Medical School building, and the oldest in the land from which the M.D. degree has been granted annually since its erection. It was put up in 1812.

MASONIC TEMPLE . . . The temple of the Ancient and Accepted Scottish Rite of Freemasonry is one of North Baltimore's imposing buildings. Completed in 1931, it gained an award as the most pleasing structure erected in the city during that year.

HAMPTON HOUSE . . . This cupolaed mansion is one of the largest of the early Maryland houses. It was built 1783-1790, and for 162 years was a Ridgely home. In 1948 it and its grounds were purchased by the Avalon Trust, which presented them to the Federal Government. It is now a National Historic Site.

BALTIMORE'S OLDEST . . . Mount Clare is that by a wide margin, for it was begun in 1754, by Charles Carroll the Barrister. In Colonial times it was the scene of much social activity; Washington and Lafayette were among the visitors there. Both this house and Hampton are open to the public.

FLAG HOUSE . . . It was in this house in 1813 that Mary Pickersgill made the fifteen-star, fifteen-stripe flag that flew over Fort McHenry during the British bombardment in 1814 and inspired Francis Scott Key to write the poem that became our national anthem. The house is now a National Historic Landmark.

OYSTER ROAST . . . What's in a name? Roast, or steamed, oysters are but one variety served up at these affairs. Raw, fried, stewed, they're wolfed in every style conceivable. Only a crab feast can match an oyster roast as a gastronomic orgy—and as a magnet for the politicians.

CHINESE PAGODA . . . This striking example of 19th Century architecture stands in Patterson Park, which has been called "East Baltimore's front yard." Designed as an observatory, the 60-foot orange and yellow pagoda is open to the public and affords an excellent view of the harbor.

DRUID HILL . . . That was the name of the great estate of Nicholas Rogers, which in 1860 became Druid Hill Park. This is the Mansion House, the home Rogers built about 1797. It now serves as the aviary and offices of the Baltimore Zoo.

CONSERVATORY . . . A showcase of brilliant colors, the conservatory and rose garden also are part of Druid Hill Park. Spring garden displays in March and April are among seasonal highlights. The conservatory is generally open from 11 to 4.

GIRAFFE HOUSE . . . One of the more modern attractions at the Baltimore Zoo in Druid Hill Park is the giraffe house. It is unique in that the giraffes are confined to an outer circle within the house and visitors, seemingly on display, view them from the center.

HISTORIC SHRINE . . . It was a flag of fifteen stars and fifteen stripes that flew over Fort Mc-Henry during the British attack of 1814 that inspired Francis Scott Key to write the poem that became our national anthem. Marines perform a military ceremony and tattoo, left, which may be witnessed Thursdays during the summer. "Soldiers" in period costumes also perform a manual of arms daily during summer months. Aerial view, below, shows the five-pointed design that makes Fort McHenry also known as the Star Fort. The flag may be flown over the fort 24 hours a day.

FORT CARROLL . . . A hexagonal island fort in the Baltimore harbor, Fort Carroll was built in 1848 and is named after Charles Carroll of Carrollton. Obsolete before it was completed, it has changed hands often and remains a monument to the past.

FORMIDABLE . . . Despite its heavy brickwork and row of cannon, never a shot was fired by Carroll's guns, although in World War II it was designated a Coast Guard pistol range. Many years later it was sold at auction for only $10,000.

FRIENDSHIP INTERNATIONAL AIRPORT . . . Capable of accommodating everything from small sport planes to the largest jets in service, Friendship ranks as one of the more modern airports in the world. It has three major runways, the longest of which is 9,500 feet, and it averages approximately 700 landings and takeoffs a day. Passenger traffic at Friendship, which is located almost midway between Baltimore and Washington, exceeds 2,000,000 annually. The airport has about 375 jet flights daily.

OLDEST WARSHIP AFLOAT . . . This distinction is held by the *Constellation*. The 38-gun frigate was launched in 1794 from David Stodder's shipyard on Harris Creek in Baltimore. She was nicknamed the "Yankee Race Horse," and was in active service through World War II, during which she was a flagship of the Atlantic Fleet. The old warship, still being restored, is at Pier 1, Pratt Street, and is open to the public. There is a nominal charge to visitors.

GRACE METHODIST . . . One of the churches that impart both beauty and dignity to Charles Street Avenue is this one of Georgian Colonial architecture with its delicate tower. The church has a set of twenty-five carillonic bells of the English type.

CATHOLIC CATHEDRAL . . . Thomas O'Neill, another of the great Baltimore merchants, left the bulk of his estate for the construction of such a church. The Cathedral of Mary Our Queen, contemporary Gothic in style, was dedicated in 1959.

UNIVERSITY BAPTIST . . . In 1921 the initial portion of this church was erected at Charles and Thirty-fourth streets. Both building and congregation have been growing steadily since, and a chapel and education center were dedicated in 1960.

OLD ST. PAUL'S . . . The Episcopal church above, at Charles and Saratoga streets, traces its history to 1692, the year the parish was founded, and it is referred to as "The Mother Parish of Baltimore." This building was dedicated in 1856, but it incorporates part of a church which was in use in 1817.

FIRST CHRISTIAN CHURCH . . . The modern house of worship below, on Roland Avenue near Lake Avenue, is a church in the round, with its altar in the center, under the steeple. The base of the steeple includes amber glass. Illuminated from within at night, the base gives off a diffused yellow light.

ST. PAUL'S RECTORY . . . Described as "an island of Georgian elegance," this rectory, with its distinctive Palladian window, was begun in 1789 and predates the present church building. Standing on land given by John Eager Howard, the rectory was financed with proceeds from a lottery.

ST. JOAN OF ARC . . . Reflecting the simplicity of many modern churches, St. Joan of Arc Catholic church in Aberdeen is perfectly square. It is just one story high, but has a large basement. Exterior walls are of dark, earth-colored bricks. The interior walls are the same color and the ceilings are gray.

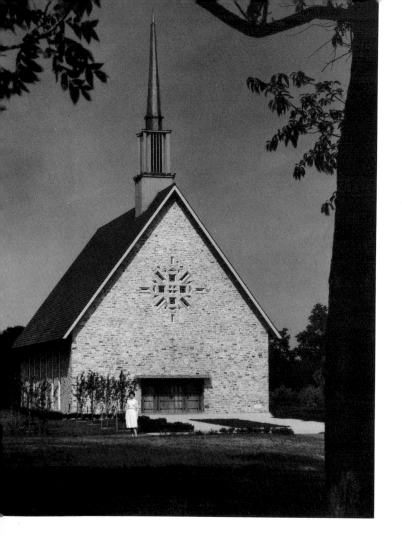

GOUCHER CHAPEL . . . Haebler Memorial Chapel, top left, at Goucher College seats 350 persons and was completed in 1963. The buff-colored exterior stone was quarried in Baltimore County. The rose window over the entrance, a memorial to Carolyn Johnston Casler, combines red, blue and green chipped glass.

OLD CATHEDRAL . . . The oldest cathedral in the United States and the mother church of Catholicism in the nation, the Minor Basilica of the Assumption of The Blessed Virgin Mary, top right, was begun in 1806 and dedicated in 1821. This Baltimore landmark stands at Cathedral and Mulberry streets.

MODERN CHURCH . . . One of the newer churches in the Baltimore area is Grace English Evangelical Lutheran Church in Lutherville. The roof is 35 feet high at the entrance and soars to 70 feet above the altar, which rests atop a huge white boulder uncovered during initial work at the site.

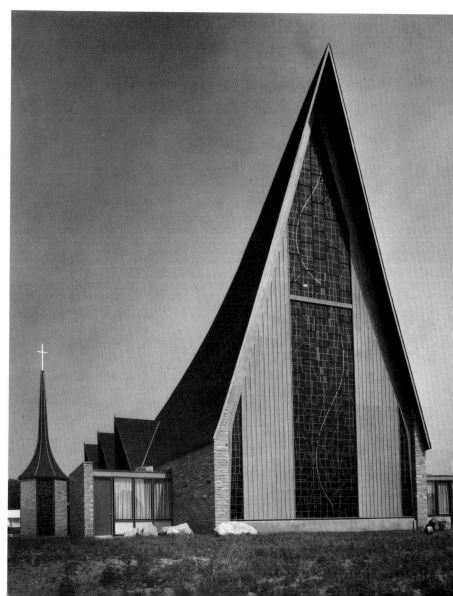

SECOND PRESBYTERIAN . . . This Georgian edifice is the
third that has been occupied by a congregation whose history goes back to 1802. The present church house and
tower were occupied in 1925, and the completed structure
was dedicated five years later. The Second Presbyterian is
also called the Guilford Community Church.

Temple Oheb Shalom . . . "Temple of the Tablets" it is sometimes called because its four arches suggest the Tablets of the Laws, or Ten Commandments. Dr. Walter Gropius, regarded by some as the father of modern architecture, designed this feature for the temple, which is one of Baltimore's many places of Jewish worship.

HAR SINAI TEMPLE . . . The great aluminum-sheathed dome rising over its sanctuary, topped by a Star of David, is 85 feet in diameter. Har Sinai is the oldest continuous reform Jewish congregation in America.

LLOYD STREET SYNAGOGUE . . . The first Jewish house of worship in Maryland, this Baltimore synagogue was built in 1845 and restored in 1964. It now serves as a museum of Jewish art and antiquities.

43

FIRST UNITARIAN . . . Because of a famous sermon the Rev. William Ellery Channing preached at the installation of its first minister in 1819, First Church is known as the birthplace of denominational Unitarianism in America. Maximilian Godefroy designed the building. The figure on the pediment is the Angel of Truth.

FRIENDS HOUSE . . . The Friends Old Town Meeting House, at Fayette and Aisquith streets, has been called Baltimore's oldest remaining house of worship. It was constructed by the Society of Friends in 1781, and it was restored in the late 1960's for use as a museum.

OLD OTTERBEIN . . . A record of use ever since it was built in 1785 makes the church at the right Baltimore's oldest in point of continuous service. Even so, it was its congregation's second. It is named for the Rev. Philip Wilhelm Otterbein, who was pastor 1774-1813, and is on Conway Street. It is Evangelical United Brethren.

CIVIC CENTER . . . Dedicated in March 1963, the Baltimore Civic Center marked something more than the opening of an entertainment center for a rapidly growing metropolitan area. It was the first building completed in Charles Center, and it signaled the start of a Baltimore renaissance. The $14,000,000 auditorium now echoes nightly to applause for performers as diverse as basketball players and guest pianists.

LYRIC THEATRE . . . Opened in 1894, the Lyric has served as Baltimore's leading concert hall for well over a half century. It seats 2,860 persons and also is the scene of ballet and opera. In the foreground of the photograph is the Maryland Line monument, which was unveiled in 1901 to honor those who fought with the Maryland Line in the Revolutionary War. Atop the granite shaft is a bronze Goddess of Liberty.

45

SPORT OF KINGS . . . Thoroughbred racing has been a popular sport in Maryland since Colonial times, and the Preakness, which is run annually at Pimlico, is the middle jewel of the Triple Crown of racing. The others in the series are the Kentucky Derby and the Belmont Stakes. The Preakness was first run in 1873.

WHERE CROWDS GATHER . . . This cavernous $14,000,-000 multi-purpose auditorium in Baltimore's Charles Center was completed in 1962. It seats more than 13,000 persons and can accommodate anything from a national convention to an ice hockey game. This scene shows the Civic Center during a track meet.

THE ORIOLES . . . Serious baseball in Baltimore has been traced to 1859, and the city has had a number of championship teams. From 1894 to 1896 it led the National League, and from 1919 to 1925 the International. In 1966 the Orioles swept the World Series by beating the Los Angeles Dodgers four games in a row.

THE COLTS . . . No Baltimore team in any sport has ever had supporters more loyal or rabid than this one's. Neither has any team repaid its backers with greater thrills. The game in which the Colts won their first National League championship in 1958 has been called the greatest football game that was ever played.

POE'S GRAVE . . . Edgar Allan Poe was buried in this cemetery, outside Old Westminster Presbyterian Church at Fayette and Greene streets, two days after he died at what is now Church Home and Hospital. Nearby, at 203 Amity Street, is the Poe House, where he lived and wrote from 1832 to 1835. The house is open Wednesdays and Saturdays.

STREETCAR MUSEUM . . . A 1902 open bench summer car and an 1880 horse-drawn car are among the items on display at this museum at 1901 Falls Road. Rides are available in several of the meticulously restored cars. The museum is open only on Sundays and hours vary with the seasons.

ANTIQUE ROW . . . This is in the 800 block of North Howard Street and has, in recent years, turned the corner into Read Street. There are more than a score of shops, with something to fascinate everyone—whether in quest of items conventional or hippy.

MOTHER SETON HOUSE . . . The small house, left, dwarfed by St. Mary's Seminary, is a shrine to Mother Seton, who is in the process of becoming the first American-born Saint of the Roman Catholic Church. She lived in the house on Paca Street when she founded the first Catholic parochial school system in this country.

FIRST OF ITS KIND . . . The first monument erected to Christopher Columbus in the New World stands at Harford Road and Parkside Drive. Dedicated in 1792, on the 300th anniversary of Columbus' voyage, it first stood at Harford Road and North Avenue. It was moved in 1963.

TRANPORTATION MUSEUM . . . The Baltimore and Ohio Railroad Museum, at Pratt and Poppleton streets, is said to house the largest collection of railroad equipment in the world. Entrance to the museum is through the first railroad passenger and freight station in the United States.

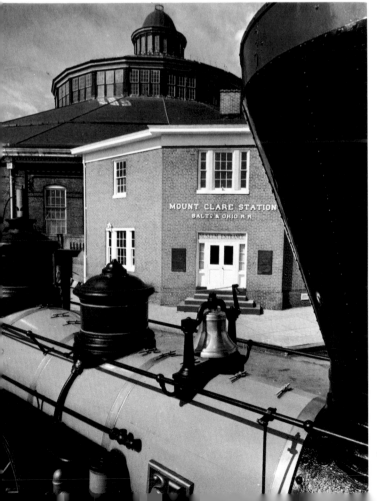

GOUCHER COLLEGE . . . Founded in 1885, and orginally the Women's College of Baltimore, this school was renamed in 1910 to honor the Rev. Dr. and Mrs. John F. Goucher, two of its founders and early benefactors. It later moved to Towson, where it has a 330-acre campus and, in 1970, could boast a 12-1 student-faculty ratio. This is Goucher College Center, with the 995-seat Kraushaar Auditorium, left, with heptagonal dome, and offices and a student service building, right.

THE MARYLAND INSTITUTE . . . When it first opened, in 1826, this was a seat of instruction in the technical and mechanical arts only. However, in 1848 a reorganization was effected, and schools of fine arts and design were added. The Institute now comprises several day and evening art schools, an evening school of drafting, and the Rinehart School of Sculpture, the last an advanced school. The spire seen at the extreme right in the photograph is that of Corpus Christi Church.

McDonogh School . . . Considered a miser while alive, John McDonogh when dead proved to be a philanthropist. He left a huge fortune for the education of children in New Orleans and Baltimore. The school above was opened in 1873. The monument on the grounds marks McDonogh's grave.

Notre Dame . . . Notre Dame has the distinction of being our country's first Catholic college for women. It opened college classes in 1895 after having been founded 48 years earlier as an academy. The building at upper right was the initial one on the present 64-acre campus, bought in 1873.

Morgan State College . . . This college began as a Bible institute in 1869. It is named for Dr. Lyttleton F. Morgan, one-time chairman of the board of trustees, whose endowment enabled it to attain college level. Founded for Negroes, it is now a State institution that attracts members of all races. Enrollment exceeds 4,300.

51

LACROSSE LEADER . . . Maryland is the nation's greatest lacrosse center, with Mount Washington perennial club champion and top American team, and Hopkins, Navy and the University of Maryland the collegiate "Big Three." Schools like St. Paul's, Gilman and Boys' Latin are training grounds. The game here is Hopkins and Yale.

GILMAN SCHOOL . . . Established in 1897 to provide "a full, well-organized day of school work, study and supervised recreation," this center of learning for boys is believed to have been the first of the country schools now numerous in the United States. It is named for Daniel Coit Gilman, one of the organizers.

WOODSTOCK COLLEGE . . . Woodstock, at top of page, was closed in 1970 when the Jesuits moved to a new campus in New York. Yet it is still remembered as another "first." It was the first scholasticate, or house of studies, for members of the Society of Jesus in our land. It was incorporated in 1867 and the first classes were held at the Maryland location in 1869. Disposition of the land and buildings was uncertain when the school closed.

ST. PAUL'S SCHOOL . . . It was as a parish day school of St. Paul's Protestant Episcopal Church, the oldest Anglican parish in Baltimore, that this institution had its beginning, well over a century ago. It occupied several locations before moving in 1952 to its present one in the Green Spring Valley. Classes range from kindergarten through college preparatory. The school provides the boys' choir for Old St. Paul's Church.

LONGSHOREMEN . . . The men unloading rubber here from a ship are longshoremen, a source of a lot of confusion among landlubbers who frequently mistake them for stevedores—the suppliers of longshoremen. The Baltimore force of longshoremen, which numbers several thousand, has an international reputation for efficiency, speed, reliability and freedom from corruption.

A GREAT PORT . . . The port and its closely allied facilities constitute the largest single industry in Baltimore. Baltimore became an important port and trading center during the Revolutionary War and achieved international recognition in the 18th Century when its speedy Clippers were bringing coffee from South America, tea from China and slaves from Africa. Now more than 100 overseas and coastal lines have some 350 general cargo sailings monthly from Baltimore.

WORLD'S BEST . . . Such is the praise given by many ship owners to launchings at the Bethlehem Sparrows Point shipyard. This great yard has several times led the globe in the amount of tonnage produced in a year. The *Gulfqueen* was one of ten 32,500-ton tankers built for the Gulf Oil Corporation.

LOCUST POINT . . . Loaded cars wait their turn to be moved alongside ships, for transfer of cargo, at one of the harbor terminals in the port of Baltimore. The railroad yards here have a capacity of nearly 3,000 cars. This is a shipping point for products from Midwestern states.

BALTIMORE HARBOR . . . A bold Inner Harbor Redevelopment Project, which is expected to cost more than $120,000,000 calls for razing many piers and buildings. They will be replaced with apartments, office buildings, a marine museum and new headquarters for the Maryland Port Authority and the Maryland Academy of Science. This view is to the southwest.

CONTAINER SHIP . . . The *M. V. Atlantic Saga,* one of the first vessels built from the keel up as a container ship, is loaded at Pier 8, Dundalk Marine Terminal. Container ships represent one of the newest concepts in world shipping, and the *Saga* has almost 2,000,000 cubic feet of cargo space.

2,000 Tons an Hour . . . At that rate, ore ships can be unloaded by the huge bridge cranes that dominate the view, above, of Port Covington, a terminal of the Western Maryland Railway. Iron ore is a principal import and moves into Baltimore at a rate exceeding 10,000,000 tons annually. Huge quantities of manganese ore and chrome ore also pass through the port.

Bananas . . . The white fleet of the United Fruit Company unloads bananas, below, at a Locust Point pier. More than 100,000 short tons of bananas are shipped to Baltimore annually from Central America for distribution over a wide area, and unloading is accomplished with the use of gantry cranes 80-feet high and conveyor belts.

76-Acre Shipyard . . . It is the one above, that of the Maryland Shipbuilding and Drydock Company at Fairfield. One of the most modern yards on the East Coast, it has facilities for repairing and converting, as well as building, all types of vessels. Thirty-two ocean-going ships can be berthed simultaneously at its five piers and in its five floating drydocks.

Biggest Tidewater Ore Dock . . . A facility of the Sparrows Point plant of Bethlehem Steel, which is the world's largest steel plant and this country's largest user of imported metallic ore, this dock is 2,200 feet long and can berth three ore ships of 60,000-ton capacity. A new 1,000-foot ore dock will accommodate ships carrying 160,000 tons of ore.

OIL AND WATER AT CANTON . . . Giant tankers lie at the piers of the Esso Standard refinery and storage site, discharging their cargoes. Both crude petroleum and petroleum products come to Baltimore from many domestic and foreign points; they comprise one of the largest bulk commodities in the port's commerce.

THE PORT WELCOME . . . This 600-passenger vessel is among the last regularly scheduled excursion boats on the Chesapeake Bay. Owned by the Maryland Port Authority and operated under a lease agreement, it offers public cruises in the summer around the port of Baltimore and to Annapolis and Betterton Beach.

EIGHTEENTH CENTURY . . . Belmont, manor house near Elkridge, was built between 1735 and 1740. The wings are believed to have been added in the early 1880's, and in 1930 the central portion was deepened. Now owned by the Smithsonian Institution, it has been designated a conference center.

THOMAS VIADUCT . . . A span of grace and beauty, this 612-foot bridge, which was begun in 1833, still carries trains over the Patapsco River. Made of granite blocks and numbering eight arches, it is a National Historic Landmark.

61

WOODLAND PATH . . . Scenery still unspoiled lines the course of the Gunpowder River as it crosses the Baltimore County countryside. The valley from Prettyboy Dam to tidewater has been urged as a State park, one that would be primarily a natural preserve, with hiking and riding trails along the river, and picnic and fishing areas.

THE FISHERMAN . . . "It could be a lake in the Maine woods" is a comment that has been made about Baltimore's Loch Raven reservoir. After the 10-mile lake was created in 1914 hundreds of thousands of pines were set out on its shores. And the Maine resemblance was again increased when in 1948 it was opened to fishing.

SUSQUEHANNA FLATS . . . Eerily bleak when ice covers them over, these shallow waters teem with life at the seasons of wildfowl migration. Thousands of geese and swans and hundreds of thousands of ducks assemble here. Ever since Colonial days the name of the Flats has been synonymous with superlative duck hunting.

HERO'S LIGHT . . . For outstanding heroism in defense of Havre de Grace when the British attacked the town in the War of 1812, John O'Neill was made keeper of the lighthouse built there in 1827, and the post was made hereditary. His descendants held it until the 1920's, when an automatic light replaced the hand-kept one.

STEEPLECHASE CLASSIC . . . The Maryland Hunt Cup ranks first among the State's three point-to-point events for gentleman riders—the others are the Grand National and My Lady's Manor. It dates to 1894. It is run in the Worthington Valley, over a four-mile course with 22 jumps. The picture above shows a finish.

ARGUMENT TO SOCIAL EVENT . . . The Hunt Cup was first run to settle an argument among five men about jumping horses. Gradually it developed into a social event, then into a spectacle. Now thousands of people gather on a hillside that forms a natural grandstand, giving an unbroken view of the race from start to finish.

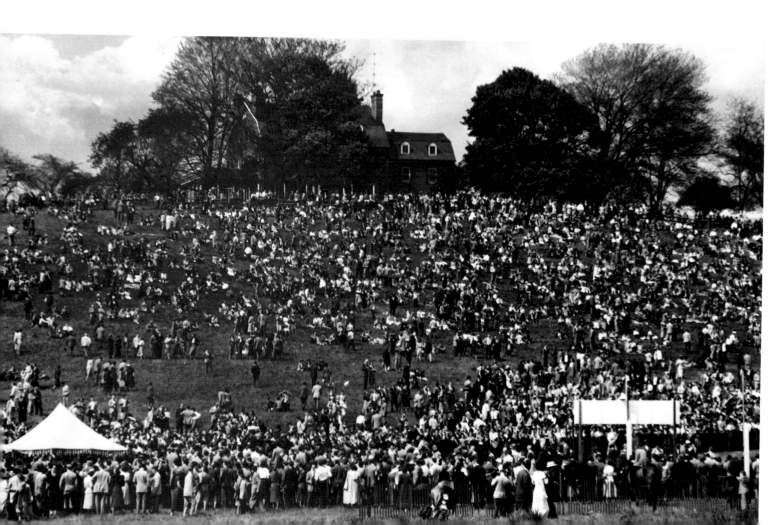

THE TIMBER RIDGE BASSETS . . . They are the first recognized pack in America. On a run they are followed afoot over miles of countryside by scores of men, women and children. Only the master of the hunt and his staff require formal attire. Rabbits are the usual quarry—but once the dogs chased a cat into a farmer's kitchen.

RIDING TO HOUNDS . . . From Maryland's earliest days the fox has provided sport for gentleman riders. A hunt held in Queen Annes County about 1650 is the first on record anywhere in America. There are nine active hunt clubs at present. The oldest is Elkridge, which was organized in 1872 and merged with Harford in 1934.

THOROUGHBRED COUNTRY . . . More than 400 horse farms dot Maryland, and they represent a charming land of white fences and winding lanes, lush meadows and gamboling foals. Merryland Farms, above, is in picturesque Long Green Valley, the heart of the horse country. Native Dancer, left, spent his last years at stud on Alfred Gwynne Vanderbilt's Sagamore Farm in Worthington Valley. He won 21 of 22 starts, earned $785,240.

HOME OF THE INTERNATIONAL . . . Laurel Race Course has attracted horse lovers since 1911, and it has become world famous for the $100,000 Washington International inaugurated at the track in 1952. The race, run annually on November 11, draws horses from more than a dozen countries, including Russia.

COLUMBIA . . . A pre-planned city in Howard County, Columbia represents an exciting new concept in living and has won numerous national honors. The first land for the ambitious project was purchased in 1962, families moved into the first of nine proposed villages in 1967, and by 1985 Columbia is expected to have a population of 110,000. More than $23,000,000 was spent on land for Columbia, where the plaza, above, overlooks a man-made lake. Below is the Merriweather Post Pavilion, which has under-cover seating for 3,000 and is the summer home of the National Symphony Orchestra. Planned as a balanced community, Columbia eventually will spread over 14,000 to 15,000 acres, or one-twelfth of the total Howard County land area. The emerging city straddles the Baltimore-Washington corridor, about 17 miles west of Baltimore.

WASHINGTON STOP . . . The tavern Col. John Rodgers opened in 1780 at Perryville was host to George Washington on many trips he made by way of the ferry there. The building now is owned by the Society for the Preservation of Maryland Antiquities.

GREY ROCK . . . The upper house at the left stands on the historic estate near Pikesville on which Col. John Eager Howard was born. It was built about 1858. It is now owned by the Trinitarian Friars, whose vocational director resides in the mansion. It is also used for meetings and retreats.

TOWN LANDMARK . . . The house the Historical Society of Carroll County occupies is one of the best-known in Westminster. It is called the Sherman-Shellman house, after the man who built it in 1807 and the town's first burgess, who once lived in it.

FARM MUSEUM . . . The Carroll County Farm Museum in Westminster once was a working farm, and the buildings, barn and smokehouse included, remain. The main building is furnished to resemble a farmhouse of the 1850's. Visitors may watch craft demonstrations, a blacksmith at work, weaving, even candlemaking. Old implements and vehicles are among the many things on exhibit.

TIDEWATER . . . Marvelously complex are the patterns of land and water along the Chesapeake's Eastern Shore. Creeks wind into the estuaries; coves and bays indent their margins; from the air the picture is bewildering. This complexity is mainly responsible for the fact that the State has a shoreline of 3,600 miles. The view at left shows the Choptank River. Right, a scene at Hoopers Island, in the heart of one of the Bay's best fishing areas.

Eastern Shore

THE MARYLAND Eastern Shore is bounded on the north by Pennsylvania, on the east by Delaware and the Atlantic Ocean, on the south by Virginia, and on the west by the Chesapeake Bay. It has more than 1,000 miles of convoluting shoreline along sounds, bays, rivers, creeks, coves and inlets—plus 32 miles of broad sand beaches on the surging Atlantic. Almost every large town on the Shore is located on navigable water.

Not much of the Shore can be seen from U.S. 50 or 301. The traveler must take the side roads that twist and turn through green fields, pine forests and along the edges of tidal marshes. Traveling these roads he will come to such lovely towns as St. Michaels and Oxford, and such villages as Honga, Bestpitch and Bivalve. If he is in no hurry, the traveler can visit churches that date from Colonial times, search out magnificent mansions that stand along the rivers, visit fishing ports, boatyards, crab pounds, seafood packing plants, chicken hatcheries, and strawberry farms. If he is lucky he may see an oyster tonger patiently at work, a log canoe racing with the wind, or a cluster of bugeyes and skipjacks moving back and forth across an oyster bed. In Maryland waters he will see more commercial sailing craft than anywhere else in America. According to Maryland law oyster dredging may be done only by sailing vessels.

The Eastern Shore is hard to describe, still harder to define. It is made up of contrasts and contradictions, both broad and subtle. As much as anything, it is a wondrous mixture of land and water, a strange blend of past and present, a way of life the outsider can envy but not really understand. Perhaps most of all, the Eastern Shore is a state of mind.

QUIET BEAUTY . . . No stream in Maryland surpasses the Choptank in loveliness, it well may be. The peace that steeps this scene—where the river forms the dividing line between Talbot and Caroline Counties—is typical of some stretches. Cambridge lies about 10 miles up from the Bay.

OLD WYE MILL . . . In about 1680 it replaced an earlier one that gave the town of Wye Mills its name. Donations and the co-operation of the Talbot Garden Club made possible its restoration in 1959. It is now owned by the Society for the Preservation of Maryland Antiquities.

SMITH ISLAND . . . The most remote of all Maryland islands, it lies west of Crisfield across Tangier Sound and is really an archipelago. Its three villages of Ewell, Rhodes Point and Tylerton are the southernmost settlements in the State. The air view shows Ewell, the largest.

WYE OAK . . . Its height of 95 feet and breadth of 165 make it the country's largest white oak, and it is the official State tree. It is over 400 years old, but in 1956 it lost its biggest limb, which weighed over 20 tons, and it is believed to be now near its end. It is at Wye Mills.

MARLIN FISHING . . . Like antennae of a giant insect, the poles stick out from the boat of a party seeking what many anglers call the king of all game fish. Its abundance in the Atlantic off Ocean City makes that place the "white marlin capital of the world."

OCEAN CITY . . . Miles of wide, white beach draw thousands upon thousands to this seaside playground each summer where, in addition to bathing, vacationers enjoy surf and deep-sea fishing, boating, golf, tennis and many other forms of sport and relaxation. Adding to the resort's growing year-round attraction is a modern $3,500,000 convention hall capable of accommodating as many as 3,700 persons for some programs. The hall, opened in 1970, is just off Sinepuxent Bay. There is a 1,000-car parking lot.

CLOSE HAULED . . . Water boils up white from the bow of the sloop *Highland Light,* a 68-footer. Beyond, running before the wind, is the 71-foot auxiliary yawl *Royono.* Both of these famed Naval Academy yachts are holders of ocean-racing records.

75

DUCK HUNTERS . . . Tidewater Maryland provides some of the finest waterfowl hunting in this country. The migration routes of many species of ducks are along the Chesapeake Bay, and the area is dotted with shooting blinds that range from the primitive to the luxurious.

NASSAWANGO FURNACE . . . Erected in 1832 to smelt iron ore from Nassawango Creek, this furnace in Worcester County once supported a thriving community. But the furnace was abandoned in 1847 and the town disappeared.

Experienced gunners usually have their decoys bobbing in the water around them as the first hues of early morning pink begin to tint the sky. Waiting patiently near most hunters there usually is a Chesapeake Bay retriever, ready to plunge into the cold water when a duck falls.

DECOY MAKER . . . Lem Ward, of Crisfield, is world famed as a decoy carver. A pair of what he calls his "fancy ducks" brings as much as $500, and he is a year and a half behind in filling orders.

SALISBURY . . . A dynamic, rapidly growing city, Salisbury is the seat of Wicomico County and a cultural, educational and medical hub for much of the Eastern Shore. Main Street shops are on the "island" formed by the Nanticoke River and multi-laned U.S. Route 50, running up from the left. An urban renewal project is in foreground.

KENT NARROWS . . . The waters of the narrows separate Kent Island from the mainland of the Eastern Shore and mark the juncture of the Chester River and Eastern Bay. The area is a center of fishing, oystering and clamming activity. The skipjack in the foreground carries seed oysters that were dredged for transplanting.

MANY-NAMED OXFORD . . . It may be that no other town in Maryland has borne as many different names as this lovely one which had its beginnings in 1668. In its earliest days it was a depot for ship supplies, including thread; this may be why it was first known as Thread Haven. Later it was called Third Haven, Tred Avon and William-Stadt before finally in 1702 becoming Oxford. For some years the town was an important port of entry, but the rapid development of Annapolis and Baltimore sent its ocean trade into eclipse. It now is a quiet hamlet that attracts many visitors from the yachting set.

BOXING SHRINE . . . Beneath a tree of which that in the foreground is a remnant was fought, in 1849, the first bare-knuckle heavyweight title bout ever held. The scene, Worton Point, Kent County, was chosen for its remoteness—boxing was then illegal. Tom Hyer beat "Yankee" Sullivan in 16 rounds for the championship and $10,000.

SPRINGFIELD FARM . . . Was erected in 1770, and stands on 600 acres of pasture and wooded land at Rock Hall. The restoration work that was done upon it in the early 1950's is authentic and has preserved all of its intimate charm. It has been called the perfect "little house."

SHIPPING CREEK . . . A date in the neighborhood of 1750 is assigned to the brick center portion of Shipping Creek Plantation, on Kent Island. The cornice of Victorian style and the frame wings are additions. The broad double portico on the front is a notable feature.

SAN DOMINGO . . . One of the early Talbot County showplaces, the Georgian mansion that bears this name was built in the years 1803-1805. Its brick was made by hand, on the place. On the grounds is the graveyard of the Harrison family, which patented the land in 1695.

BLAKEFORD . . . A showcase, which was destroyed by fire in 1970, was the main house on the 1,400-acre estate, near Queenstown, of Mr. and Mrs. Clarence W. Miles. The magnificent house overlooked the Chester River. With Mrs. Miles here are the Duke and Duchess of Windsor.

BOHEMIA . . . This Georgian house, built about 1745 and restored to its present condition, stands on the south fork of the Bohemia River south of Chesapeake City. Benjamin Franklin was a guest there on numerous occasions; his visits are corroborated by written history, including his *Autobiography*.

TALBOT COURTHOUSE . . . The central portion of the building dates to 1794. It was restored, and the wings were added, several years ago in keeping with a project to return the entire courthouse square to the appearance it had in Easton's early days, when Colonial and Georgian architecture predominated.

STINTON . . . Among Kent Island's historic homes is this one, parts of which were erected in 1700. Even though it had been neglected for years before new owners began repairs, many markings survived that proved its age. A foundation made of cedar stumps testifies to the lack of rock faced by the builders.

TRINITY CHURCH . . . It is one of the three oldest in the United States still in its original form, judging from records which show that it was already established in 1690. It stands on the bank of a quiet little Dorchester County stream to which it has given the name of Church Creek.

ALL HALLOWS . . . Little change has been made in the exterior of this Snow Hill church in all the 200 years and more since it was built, though there has been some remodeling of the interior. Two treasures of the congregation are a Bible and a bell that were presented by Queen Anne.

GREEN HILL . . . From Colonial times until about the Civil War, St. Bartholomew's—the true name of this church on the Wicomico River—was in regular use. Then it was abandoned till the 1890's, when it was repaired to be opened for one service annually. The annual service is still held.

OLD WYE CHURCH . . . One of the interior features of St. Luke's Episcopal Church—which is Old Wye's true name—is more unusual than its exterior. It has box pews with benches for worshippers on three sides and a door on the fourth. The first Episcopal services in Maryland are believed to have been conducted, in 1631, near its site on the old Queenstown-Easton road. A church to which a date of 1650 is attributed preceded the present one, which was opened in 1721. Restoration work was done here in 1949, and the parish house at left was built in 1957, through the generosity of Mr. and Mrs. Arthur A. Houghton, Jr.

A School Ship . . . The full-rigged ship about to pass under the Chesapeake Bay Bridge, years before construction of a parallel span, is the *Danmark*. For many years Danish merchant marine officers were trained on her. During World War II thousands of American seamen also were trained on her.

MENDING THE NET . . . When they are not catching fish or selling fish Chesapeake watermen are likely to be found either drying or mending their nets. It is a daily chore. Some of the men do the work with needles they carved themselves from hardwood.

CHESAPEAKE OYSTERMAN . . . As he stands at the wheel of his skipjack, toughened and bronzed by exposure to wind and weather, Captain Orville Parks, of Cambridge, typifies the Maryland waterman. He has been an oyster dredger in the Bay and its rivers for well over half a century, and in all that time he has never wrecked a boat, turned one over, or carried off a mast. He sails for pleasure, too, and is the undisputed sailing champion of the Bay, having skippered his boat *Rosie* to an unequaled number of victories in workboat races off Sandy Point and elsewhere. His view of his occupation is typical, too: "I like the water business. It's a nice living; a good clean living. We've had some tough times, but we're not starving. We send our children to school and pay our bills. My credit's good in any store in town."

CLAMMER . . . Generations of baymen looked on the mannino, or soft-shell clam, as trash. Nowadays, though, thousands of bushels are sold to New England for its famous clambakes. A dredge loosens the clams from the muddy bottom with jets of water, and a conveyer belt draws them up.

CRAB POUND . . . In the spring, the blue crab's fancy turns to thoughts of a roomier shell, and when crabs shed their old, hard carapaces, they become succulent "soft crabs." Growing crabs are confined in floats during this transition, and 300,000 crabs a year pass through the floats of this crab pound in Crisfield.

LOW SKIES, HIGH SPIRITS . . . "Fair weather's our worst enemy," an oyster dredger will tell you. "We'll sit two days out of five on the average, when we could be working, because there isn't enough wind to let us pull a drudge. When it's blowin' and snowin', that's when you got to be out there." The reason for this is that the law prohibits dredging—or drudging, as the watermen pronounce it—from power boats; oysters can be taken in this way only from craft using sail.

SHELL GAME . . . Great mounds of shells like that at the right are the sign of an oyster packing plant. This one is on Deals Island, in Tangier Sound. Directly or indirectly, the entire populace there makes its living by catching, packing and shipping oysters and crabs, trapping muskrats, and taking out parties of anglers. Oyster shells were once a common road-building material in Maryland; now they are "planted" back in the water for young oysters to attach to.

WOMAN'S WORK . . . Usually, on a tonging boat, it is that of sorting the oysters and throwing back the tiny ones. But some of the wives who go out with their men also use the 22-foot tongs with which the catch is brought up—though when filled these can weigh as much as 50 pounds.

POUND NETTERS . . . This type of net is large and square; it is closed at the bottom and its upper edges are tied to stakes which hold them above water. Funnel-shaped nets lead into it beneath the surface, and fish entering these are trapped in the main "pound." The men above are working with a net of this type.

HAUL SEINERS . . . Their net, 750 feet long and weighted at the bottom, is dropped from a boat around an observed school of fish, or at a likely location, and then the ends are drawn in tighter and tighter. It is strenuous work, but the three generations of a family here doing it in Lankford Bay include a 17-year-old girl.

THE HERRING RUN . . . A majority of the more than 200 kinds of fish that are native to the Chesapeake are found in Maryland's waters. At the mouth of the Susquehanna River the spring run of herring provides one of the big catches, and it was during this that these fishermen had set up their pound net.

CONOWINGO . . . As seen from Port Deposit, the great
dam and hydroelectric plant stretch impressively across
the wide Susquehanna River. The dam is 4,648 feet long
and 105 feet high. It backs up the river for more than
14 miles into a deep lake that contrasts sharply with the
shallows pictured.

C & D CANAL . . . Since 1829 the Chesapeake and Delaware Canal has linked the bays of those names, first as
a lock canal and now as a toll-free free-flow one. It annually records more than 22,000 vessel passings and is
busier than either the Panama Canal or the Suez Canal.
The photograph shows Chesapeake City.

FADING INTO HISTORY . . . The *Jennie D. Bell,* the last ram to sail the Bay, rots away on the flats of the Wicomico River off Nancy Point, near Salisbury. Rams originated in Bethel, Delaware, and the *Jennie D.* was built in 1898. As late as 1957 she carried grain to Baltimore.

SAILING NO MORE . . . The *J. T. Leonard,* here used for oystering, was the last sloop in commerical service in Bay waters. She was retired and now is on display at the Chesapeake Bay Maritime Museum in St. Michaels. The only boat of her gaff-rigged type, she was built in 1882.

CRISFIELD . . . "Seafood Capital of the Country" it is called. Craft like the outermost three bring it for packing and sale thousands of tons of delicacies from the lower Bay area. The two boats at right link Smith and Tangier Islands with the mainland.

IT'S AN ILL WIND . . . That blows no good, as Ocean City will testify. In 1933 a hurricane gouged a channel between its Sinepuxent Bay and the ocean and turned its minor fishing industry into a major one. This is one of the commercial fishing docks.

SAND AND SEA . . . A barrier reef over 20 miles long, Assateague Island is being developed as a National Seashore, and just beyond the bridge from the mainland is a State Park that annually attracts thousands who enjoy the excellent fishing and swimming.

MUSKRATS . . . Thousands of them are trapped yearly in Eastern Shore marshes. The meat is sold as "marsh rabbit." The fur sometimes becomes "Hudson seal." A skinning contest is held annually at Cambridge and draws entrants from as far as Louisiana.

PORT OF CAMBRIDGE . . . Workmen unload frozen cod and haddock brought from Iceland aboard the vessel *Bruarfoss*. Cambridge, like Baltimore, is a deep-water port capable of accommodating large ocean-going vessels, and much of the ship traffic involves frozen fish imported from Iceland for processing in Maryland and distribution.

The Cambridge Marine Terminal, which cost $1,100,000, was completed in 1963. The port promptly developed a substantial business in frozen fish, with 15,000 tons moving through the harbor in 1964. Soon the figure had more than doubled, and in calendar 1969, a total of 36,000 tons of frozen fish passed through the busy terminal.

BROILER HOUSE . . . This broiler house in Salisbury, in the heart of the Delmarva poultry region, is fully automated. It produces 275,000 broiler chickens annually that receive their feed and water automatically. Even the lights go on and off automatically.

GOURMET'S DELIGHT . . . The crab and the oyster vie for the title, and it is unlikely that there will ever be a decision between them. Picking the meat from crabs for packing is still chiefly a hand operation, although a machine to do it has been devised. Women pickers work at tables covered with stainless metal, as at the right. Below, a trayful of live soft crabs on the way to market.

ACRES OF STRAWBERRIES . . . Marion Station, in
Somerset County, is the heart of an immense strawberry producing area. Every year, in May, hundreds
of thousands of dollars' worth of the fruit is brought
here for auction. The region also supplies some
50,000,000 young plants annually to growers elsewhere in Maryland and in states to the north.

ACRES OF POTATOES . . . So many acres, in the southernmost portion of Worcester County, that tractor-drawn machinery like that below is used to dig up the crop. Field hands follow the diggers, when the clouds of dust have settled, and gather up the potatoes before the sun can damage them. The dark, sandy loam and the climate of this area have proved particularly favorable for early varieties.

GREEN GOLD . . . Tobacco is that to the five southern counties of Maryland. The type produced is one of the finest grown anywhere in the world, and from 150,000 to 200,000 acres are regularly devoted to it. It is the staple upon which about 6,000 planters and their families depend.

SOMETHING OLD . . . "Windowless windows" on the barns are a tradition in several counties, and particularly in the Montgomery County area that embraces Sandy Spring, Ashton and Olney. The painting is usually white on a dark background, and the pattern a bold, simplified one.

STRIKING SILHOUETTE . . . In 1939 a number of Amish families from Pennsylvania moved to St. Marys County. They prospered and their number has grown. Thus, today, it is not unusual to see them on country roads traveling to or from market in horse-drawn wagons.

Southern Maryland

SOUTHERN Maryland embraces five counties—Anne Arundel, Prince Georges, Calvert, Charles, St. Marys—and a manner of life all its own. Away from north-south U.S. 301 and burgeoning urban areas, life is essentially rural, leisurely, with emphasis on family, good living and a sense of the past.

Within its boundaries lie the ancient and lovely city of Annapolis, the United States Naval Academy, the first seat of government in Maryland, a school and college that date to the 18th Century, some of the finest Colonial homes in the State, the Patuxent Naval Air Test Center, the Calvert Cliffs which are one of the best hunting grounds for marine Miocene fossils in North America, and such places as Half Pone Point, Point-No-Point, Horsehead, TB, and Burnt Store.

Tobacco is the main crop on this tidewater coastal plain, and has been since recorded history in Maryland began. Southern Maryland tobacco is prized by America's cigarette makers for its aroma, taste and free burning qualities.

Queen city of this country is Annapolis, named in honor of a princess who became Queen Anne. Annapolis, which is almost surrounded by water, is many things—county seat, trading center, college town, pleasure boat port, State capital, home of the Naval Academy, and, in the words of one authority, "The most perfect example of a Colonial city extant in America today."

Southern Maryland is changing as Washington suburbs push outward, urban communities mushroom around Government installations, and the shores of the Potomac, the Patuxent and Chesapeake Bay become a playland for Washington and Baltimore. Despite these changes, Southern Maryland still retains its charm, its distinctive way of life, and old world air.

ANNAPOLIS SKYLINE . . . As viewed from City Dock, at the foot of Main Street, the skyline is dominated by the dome of the State House and the spire of St. Anne's Episcopal Church. In foreground is a fleet of skipjacks, part of the last commercial sailing fleet in the United States.

GOVERNMENT HOUSE . . . The executive mansion is an imposing mid-Victorian building that dates to 1867. The end chimneys, broad gables, Palladian windows and flanking wings were added in 1936. The residence of Maryland governors again underwent extensive renovation in 1967.

STATE HOUSE . . . The imposing, domed landmark, right, is the oldest state capitol in the nation still used for legislative purposes. The building was begun in 1772, and two others preceded it on the site. The statue at the entrance is that of Roger Brooke Taney, former Chief Justice of the United States.

OLD SENATE CHAMBER . . . This room in the State House was the scene of great events. The United States Congress met here from November 16, 1783, to June 3, 1784. In this room Washington presented his resignation as commander-in-chief of the Continental Army. The Treaty of Paris was ratified here.

PACA GARDENS . . . The elaborate gardens of William Paca, Maryland's third governor, were begun about 1765. They were reputed to be among the most beautiful in Colonial America. Restored in 1970, after having been hidden beneath debris, they bloom again in Annapolis.

HALL OF RECORDS . . . Housed in the building above are archives of the State and its counties that in some cases date back to Maryland's founding as a colony. The Hall was built in 1934, on a corner of the St. John's College campus, as a memorial to the tercentenary of that founding.

OLD TREASURY . . . The modest structure at the right is the oldest public building in the State. It was erected 1735-1737 for the issuance of paper money, later became a council chamber, then from the mid-1800's to 1903 was used by the State Treasurer.

LIBERTY TREE . . . Revolutionary meetings held at it gained this name for the great tulip poplar, which is believed to be over 600 years old and is 29 feet around. A treaty with Indians is said to have been signed under it in 1652. The tree stands in front of Woodward Hall, the library building of St. John's College.

NOON FORMATION . . . The brigade of Midshipmen assembles at Bancroft Hall, the building from which all activity at the Naval Academy radiates. It houses all 4,200 of the men, and its mess hall can serve them all at a single sitting. It is said to be the largest dormitory in the world; there are three miles of corridors.

TECUMSEH . . . A bronze copy of the figurehead from the *U.S.S. Delaware*, Tecumseh is known as the "God of c," which is the passing grade. Midshipmen frequently toss pennies at Tecumseh for good luck. Nearby on the grounds of the Naval Academy is Bancroft Hall, said to be the largest dormitory in the world.

DRESS PARADE . . . The highlight of the year at the Naval Academy is June Week, when graduates receive their commissions. One of the colorful traditions of the week is a dress parade on Worden Field when the old color company transfers the American and regimental flags to a new company chosen in year-long competition.

BRICE HOUSE . . . Not only do its wings with their connecting hyphens make it an excellent example of the distinctive Maryland Georgian mansion, but in it Annapolis has one of the finest specimens of Colonial architecture extant, experts say. It is variously dated 1740 to 1773.

CHASE-LLOYD . . . Its height of three stories is rare for its period —it was begun by Samuel Chase, a Signer of the Declaration of Independence, in 1769, and completed by Edward Lloyd about 1774. Here Mary Tayloe Lloyd became the bride of Francis Scott Key in 1802.

PLANNED CAPITAL . . . Streets in Annapolis radiate from State Circle and Church Circle, as an aerial view shows. Ours is the only State capital that was deliberately laid out in Colonial days primarily as a seat of government. The stream here is Spa Creek; across it, Eastport.

ST. ANNE'S . . . In 1692 its parish was established; it is the third church on the site. An altar tomb contains the remains of Sir Robert Eden, the last Provincial Governor. On left, the 1737 Reynolds Tavern; it is now the Public Library of Annapolis and Anne Arundel County.

THE AMISH . . . Six families of these farmers led
the migration from Pennsylvania to St. Marys County
in 1939; now there are more than 50 families. One of
their market places is on a seven-acre tract lying beside
State Route 5, three miles south of Hughesville. Market days have been Wednesday and Saturday.

SCHOOL DAYS . . . For Amish boys they are usually short; too much education breeds laziness, their elders hold. At about the age of 14 most of the youngsters are taken from class and put to work in the fields. The boys pictured were enjoying recess outside their Newmarket school.

PLAIN PEOPLE . . . "Our dress is just a sign of our religion," the Amish say. The women wear solid colors—blue, purple, lavender, green, gray, brown. The gauzy prayer cap is worn both indoors and under the outdoor bonnet, because: "St. Paul tells us to pray without ceasing."

FRANCIS SCOTT KEY
FITZGERALD
SEPTEMBER 24. 1896
DECEMBER 21. 1940
HIS WIFE
ZELDA SAYRE
JULY 24. 1900
MARCH 10. 1948

THE JAZZ AGE . . . Not only was it depicted with brilliance in the novels and short stories that F. Scott Fitzgerald wrote; it was epitomized in his life. Rockville Cemetery, on the old Columbia Pike, Route 28, is the resting place of the author of "The Great Gatsby," "This Side of Paradise" and other chronicles of the 1920's.

GREAT FALLS . . . In the cataracts of the Potomac, shown in the picture at upper left, Montgomery County has one of our State's finest scenic attractions. Potholes like that in the foreground of the view pit the rocks. The area is a State Park, with recreational facilities and several historic sites adding to its interest.

CALVERT CLIFFS . . . Famous for the number and variety of marine fossils that are found in them, the cliffs edge the Chesapeake for 30 miles in Calvert County, rising 100 feet high in places. Fossils are from sharks, birds, mollusks and other animals that lived in the Miocene period, about 16,000,000 years ago. In sharp contrast to the distant past is a $380,000,000 nuclear-fueled generating plant, which the Baltimore Gas and Electric Company is building at Calvert Cliffs. The two-unit, 800-kilowatt plant is expected to be completed by 1974.

GREAT FALLS TAVERN . . . It has
stood for over a century and a quarter at Lock 20 of the Chesapeake &
Ohio Canal. At present one room is
a museum; exhibits tell the story of
the 185-mile waterway, which in part
or whole was in service 1831-1924.
The canal is now Federally owned,
and a parkway along it is being urged.

YESTERYEAR REVISITED . . . The 60-
passenger barge *John Quincy Adams,*
which went into operation in 1967,
carries passengers over a four-mile seg-
ment of the Chesapeake and Ohio
Canal in much the same manner as
barges plied the waterway in the last
century. The barge is boarded at Great
Falls.

113

UNIVERSITY OF MARYLAND . . . On its 1,400-acre main campus at College Park, the third largest main campus in the United States, are more than 200 buildings, many designed in the Georgian Colonial style. The university has more than 82,000 students here and overseas with a teaching staff which exceeds 6,000. It is a land-grant institution, and the College of Engineering, in tribute to the man whose gifts helped make it possible, is called the Glenn L. Martin Institute of Technology. The university grew out of two schools—a medical school organized in Baltimore in 1807, and the Maryland Agricultural College, chartered at College Park in 1856.

SILVER SPRING . . . The glitter of mica sand in its water, on a sunny day in 1840, led its discoverers to call it that, and in time the name was conferred also on the community that grew up around the Montgomery County spot. Some years ago, after the site of the spring had been included in a park, it was restored as shown.

McKELDIN LIBRARY . . . The Theodore R. McKeldin Library at the University of Maryland now holds more than 1,000,000 books, and it has room for many more. Its reading rooms seat 2,000, and it has 100 carrels and 30 enclosed studies. There also are various rooms for conferences and seminars.

U. S. NAVAL HOSPITAL . . . There are few medical centers in the world as large and well-equipped as this one on the Rockville Pike near Bethesda. Its staff not only ministers to the ill and wounded, but trains physicians and dentists and does much research. It has within its walls all the facilities of a small civilian community.

MONTPELIER . . . Thomas Snowden began work in 1740 on the 22-room red brick Colonial mansion, top, at Bowie, in Prince Georges County. The two wings were added in 1771. In 1965 a developer bought much of the land around Montpelier, but the mansion was to be refurbished and preserved as a showplace.

LA PLATA COURTHOUSE . . . Both the old and the new are combined in this landmark in the Charles County seat. The original La Plata Courthouse was built in 1896, and much of it was retained when it was transformed into the building, above, in 1955. Its serpentine wall duplicates one Jefferson designed for the University of Virginia.

FORT WASHINGTON . . . The lighthouse and fort pictured here stand on the site of the earliest fortification erected for defense of the nation's capital. They are on the Maryland shore of the Potomac River, just opposite Mount Vernon. The first fort on the site was completed in 1809 and destroyed by the British in 1814. Fort Washington as it exists today was finished in 1824. During the Civil War, troops from the 4th Artillery and other units manned the fort. It was abandoned in 1872, and then from 1896 to 1921 it was headquarters for the Defenses of the Potomac. Recently restored by the National Park Service, it is now open to the public.

BUREAU OF STANDARDS . . . Maryland is the home of one of the finest physical science laboratories in the world. It is the 560-acre National Bureau of Standards complex in Gaithersburg. At left is the administration building.

117

AIR-CURING TOBACCO . . . Maryland tobacco is one of only two varieties used in cigarettes that are air-cured; the other is Kentucky burley. The cut stalks are hung up like this in barns that have ventilators, or doors, in their sides; through these the tobacco is visible as it slowly dries. Such air-curing takes several months, in contrast to flue-curing, which is done in a few days. The characteristics that make Maryland tobacco especially valuable are that it is bright, mellow—that is, low in nicotine—chaffy and fine, so that it gives more bulk per pound, and fast-burning. It is the driest tobacco that is produced anywhere.

CHARLOTTE HALL SCHOOL . . . Is older than our Republic, for it was chartered in 1774 and named for Queen Charlotte of England. Only during the Revolution were its classes suspended; it operated continuously since 1796 and has been a military academy since about 1797. It is in Charlotte Hall, Maryland.

SMALLWOOD'S RETREAT . . . This little Charles County house was built by Maj.-Gen. William Smallwood as a home after his valorous service in the Revolution. Smallwood also was a Governor of Maryland, from 1785 to 1788. In 1958 the house was restored and made a museum in a 300-acre State Park.

WASHINGTON DANCED . . . And Benjamin Franklin played the musical glasses, tradition says, during one gay evening in the mansion above. It is Whitehall, near Annapolis, built in 1765 as the home of Horatio Sharpe, Royal Governor. It has been pronounced "one of America's truly great Colonial residences."

CLOCKER'S FANCY . . . The brick central part of the St. Marys County house below is of a date earlier than 1681. Daniel Clocker, who in 1649 patented its site, was a servant of a Captain Cornwallis, and his wife a servant of the famed Margaret Brent, the first American woman to seek equal legal rights with men.

SEAT OF GOVERNMENT . . . When in the 1650's the Puritans seized control of the Colony from Lord Baltimore's men, the Calvert County house above became their capitol. Originally called Preston-on-Patuxent, it is better known as Charles' Gift, the name given it by author Hulbert Footner, a recent owner.

TULIP HILL . . . The garden front, which overlooks West River and the Chesapeake, is the side pictured. The house was erected in 1756—the pierced chimneys are uncommon for that time—and named for the tulip poplars that abounded on the property. In his diary George Washington recorded several visits here.

Western Maryland

WESTERN Maryland is the clustered spires of Frederick . . . the rounded mounds of the Alleghenies, blue and purple from a distance . . . the rich valleys of Frederick, Middletown and Hagerstown . . . Conococheague Creek passing under ancient stone arches . . . a sweeping bend of the Potomac . . .

Western Maryland is limestone dotted meadows . . . stone fences laced with honeysuckle . . . a community butchering on a fall morning . . . a porchful of pumpkins . . . the geometric patterns of apple orchards on a hillside . . . maple sugaring . . . pulpwood forests . . . and strip mining . . .

Western Maryland reaches into the past . . . back to the days of the Ohio Company's trading posts . . . the French and Indian wars . . . General Braddock's march into the wilderness . . . young George Washington's military campaigns . . . the start of the National Road from Cumberland . . . the Chesapeake & Ohio Canal which carried coal to Georgetown . . .

Western Maryland has the highest altitude in the state, 3,340 feet on Backbone Mountain . . . at Hancock the narrowest part of Maryland . . . coldest section in winter . . . . coolest spot in summer . . . winter wonderland . . . summer vacation area . . . trout streams . . . Deep Creek Lake . . . virgin forest of white pine and hemlock . . . misty waterfalls . . . beautiful scenery.

TOP OF THE STATE . . . At 3,095 feet, Table Rock, on Backbone Mountain in Garrett County, is the highest spot on any Maryland road. It is shown in the upper photo on the opposite page. In the lower view, also a Garrett County one, Winding Ridge is seen from Negro Mountain. The latter is so called because in the 1700's a Negro member of a military force was killed there by Indians.

MASON-DIXON MARKER . . . Every mile along the Maryland-Pennsylvania line they surveyed in the years 1763 to 1767, Charles Mason and Jeremiah Dixon planted a stone with M carved on the south side and P on the north. And every five miles they set a stone with coats of arms incised. This is one of those "crown stones."

STATE'S REFRIGERATOR . . . Weather like this earns Western Maryland the designation. At the time the picture was taken, a 60-mile wind was piling up drifts on the heels of a blizzard. The location is Meadow Mountain in Garrett County, and the view is from Route 40 toward Grantsville. The altitude here is 2,789 feet.

BLACK ROCK CLIFFS . . . Giving a spectacular view over forested South Mountain and the farmlands of Frederick County that lie off in the distance, they are one of the Maryland attractions on the Appalachian Trail. That is the 2,050-mile hiking route which runs between Mount Katahdin in Maine and Mount Oglethorpe, Ga.

MOUNT AIRY . . . An unusual water tank marks from afar this town on the Carroll-Frederick county line. It is called a single-stem spheroid and is about 125 feet high. To some it resembles a gigantic golf ball on a tee.

125

CLUSTERED SPIRES . . . Whittier characterized well one of the striking features of Frederick. Left to right in this view, the steeples and cupolas are: Visitation Convent; St. John's Catholic Church (gleaming tip barely visible); Courthouse; Evangelical Reformed; Evangelical Lutheran; Trinity Chapel; All Saints Episcopal.

COFFMAN CHAPEL . . . The edifice above, on the Hood College campus in Frederick, is named in honor of Mr. and Mrs. Andrew K. Coffman, benefactors of the institution. Hood was established in 1893 as the Woman's College of Frederick, and renamed in 1913 in tribute to Margaret E. S. Hood.

BAKER MEMORIAL . . . This chapel was dedicated in 1958 at Western Maryland College in Westminster. Its name is a recognition of gifts by William G. Baker, Jr., in honor of his family, which went far toward making its erection possible. The college, which is a coeducational one, dates to 1868.

THE HAGER HOUSE . . . Although most of the early houses in the State are on the Eastern Shore and in Southern Maryland, one of the oldest of our restorations is the home of Jonathan Hager, founder of Hagerstown. The major part of it was built about 1740; some portions are even older. The house stands above two springs, which still well up in the basement.

STONE FENCES . . . Typical of both the Middletown and Cumberland valleys, they are made from rocks gathered from the adjacent fields. Those pictured are just one of several varieties. Some are over a century old and were used as ramparts when the Civil War swept over the region.

STRIP MINING . . . Midlothian in Allegany County is the scene of the operation. Strip mining is the digging of coal from the surface, rather than from underground shafts. The seam here is the Georges Creek, which yields a famous grade of fuel. Garrett County is also a coal producer.

FIVE ARCHES . . . Many stone bridges notable for grace of line and beauty of masonry are to be seen in the State's western sections. The one that crosses Conococheague Creek at Cearfoss in Washington County has still another eye-catching feature in the number of its spans.

COLLECTORS' MECCA . . . The last quarter-century has seen the town of New Market, in Frederick County, earn a reputation as a place to visit for antiques. At last count, the town had 31 antique shops stocked with items as diverse as porcelain and airplane propellers. One can find china and crystal, paintings and period furniture, brass and old books, even some items the dealers cannot identify.

MAPLE SUGARING . . . Surely the most romantic of all Western Maryland activities, it traditionally begins the week of Washington's Birthday and continues until the buds of the trees start to swell—late March or early April. Three-inch tubes known as spiles are driven into the trees; through them the "maple water" flows into four-gallon buckets, or keelers, hung from them. Tank carts like that in the picture collect the sweet liquid and take it to a "camp" where it is boiled down to syrup and sugar. An average tree yields 40 to 50 gallons of sap, and some groves are as large as 90 acres. The present scene is Garrett County.

BUTCHERING . . . It is still a country art. In this instance it was done by members of the Ruritan Club of Burkittsville; they killed a number of hogs they had raised to help finance their service projects. They sold not only meat cuts, but pudding, sausage and lard that they made.

SUGAR LOAF MOUNTAIN . . . This is the view, looking south, from the 1,281-foot summit of a mountain that is a Registered Natural Landmark. It is considered a geological puzzle, standing as it does at the gateway to Western Maryland's Catoctin Mountains—yet separate from the Appalachians. Federal troops were entrenched on the Frederick County mountain during the Civil War. It was from Sugar Loaf that Robert E. Lee's army was spotted as it crossed the Potomac at White's Ford.

DOE GULLY . . . That is the colorful name of the place where this Western Maryland Railway train crosses the Potomac River from Maryland into West Virginia. In the background is Green Ridge Mountain, in Allegany County. The rugged terrain here necessitates a maximum of power; each of the three diesel units of the train is a 1,500-horsepower one. Even so, the grades between this point and Baltimore, and especially those around Blue Ridge Summit, limit trains to 65 loaded cars.

OLD CROSSINGS . . . Time was when the State had more than half a hundred of the picturesque covered bridges. Today it has eight. The uppermost of the three shown is at Loys Station, on the Utica Mills county road about 15 miles north of Frederick. Its two spans are each 45 feet in length.

THE LONGEST . . . Our remaining bridges are scattered over several sections of the State. The one at the immediate right, which is the largest still standing, is in Cecil County. Its single span is a 119-foot one. It takes a county road over Northeast Creek half a mile north of Bay View.

BOWSTRING ARCH . . . A bridge across Big Elk Creek northeast of Fair Hill, also in Cecil County, is of the beautiful bowstring arch type, but its arches are unusual. They are made of straight timbers bolted together, instead of long beams laboriously bent. This one is on private duPont property.

133

700 LILY PONDS . . . Square, shallow and set at staggered levels like rice paddies, they give a Chinese look to a hillside 10 miles south of Frederick. They mark the world's largest rearing place of exotic water plants and ornamental fish — Lilypons, named for the famous singer.

PIE IN THE SKY . . . When the frost's been on the punkin there are scenes like this on Western Maryland farms as the housewife picks out the ones she wants before sending the rest to market. But in the left background there is also one that seems likely to become a jack-o'-lantern.

134

AN APPLE A DAY . . . Would get you nowhere at all in face of the big Washington County crop. There are 77,000 trees in one orchard alone, and altogether the State's production comes near 1,500,000 bushels yearly.

A HARD NUT . . . To crack—is a phrase that describes both the hickory and the black walnut, but this Washington Countian cracks them both for his tobacco money. He picks out the meats with a nail and sells them to stores.

MARYLAND GOTHIC . . . Grant Wood's celebrated oil "American Gothic" is recalled by the portrait at right of two brothers, then 72 and 75, with one of the Belgian horses they used on their farm in Washington County.

135

GREEN GOLD . . . The phrase that in Southern Maryland means tobacco, in Western Maryland means pulpwood. One-tenth of the State's annual wood harvest is now being sold to the pulp and paper industry. Forests are being farmed as carefully as fields, especially on marginal-quality land.

C. & O. LOCK 52 . . . The quiet beauty of the Hancock section of the old waterway is typical of the whole, and is the quality that makes the historic towpath a mecca for hikers—one they hope will be preserved. In the canal's heyday 750 barges plied between Cumberland and Georgetown.

FISHIN' AND FIDDLIN' . . . Western Maryland, with its mountainous terrain and demanding winters, produces hardy people. The heavily bundled native samples ice fishing at Deep Creek Lake. Bachelor Edward Moore relaxes on his Allegany County farmstead where he has lived 83 years as a relatively self-sufficient mountaineer.

PULP AND PAPER MILL . . . The largest mill of the West Virginia Pulp and Paper Company, pictured here, is in Luke, Maryland, at the southwestern tip of Allegany County. The company also has a development laboratory at Luke, and in 1966 it opened a $1,500,000 research center in Howard County.

EARTH'S BOUNTY . . . Setting the scene of "Barbara Frietchie" in 1863, Whittier wrote of Frederick County's "meadows rich with corn." A century later his words still apply. Frederick is the State's leading county in the production of corn and cattle and in quantity of dairy products.

CROOKED TREES . . . Their unusual shapes accentuated by the snow striping their sides, they make a picture that has won prizes in shows all over the world — Australia, France, South Africa, Brazil, Hong Kong, to name only a few of the places. The trees grow on Backbone Mountain.

138

TRI-STATE VIEW . . . Three states can be seen in this picture, which was made from Lovers Leap in West Virginia. It is near Hancock, at a point where Maryland is narrowest or only four miles wide. Flowing beneath the craggy rocks is the Potomac River. Bordering the river is the Chesapeake and Ohio Canal. Then comes a railroad, and beyond that lie the National Pike and the rolling hills of Pennsylvania. The Potomac in this section of Maryland is a favorite among canoeists. The Chesapeake and Ohio Canal, which is under the jurisdiction of the National Park Service, attracts thousands annually who enjoy hiking and cycling on the towpath.

COLONIAL BARRACKS . . . Erected about 1750 as a protection against Indian raids, the gray stone building is on the grounds of the Maryland School for the Deaf at Frederick. During the Revolutionary War it was either repaired or enlarged for use as a prison, and became the place of detention for British soldiers taken in the Battles of Saratoga, Trenton and Yorktown. Here also were held French seamen from the frigate *L'Insurgente,* captured by the *U.S.F. Constellation*—the first capture made by the American Navy, in 1799. Again during the War of 1812 it saw such use, for British prisoners taken at Bladensburg.

MUSEUM OF FINE ARTS . . . A gift to Hagerstown and Washington County from Anna Brugh Singer, wife of the painter William H. Singer, Jr., it stands beside a lake in City Park. Sculpture, painting and the graphic arts are all represented in its permanent collection, and its staff does much educational work.

DIP NETTING . . . It's an old manner of fishing that is practiced mainly along the Potomac and the Susquehanna. Every evening, in spring and early summer, dip netters are busy on these rivers. The Potomac yields them crappies, yellow suckers, sunfish, catfish, sometimes carp; the Susquehanna herring, shad and perch.

FORT FREDERICK . . . Built by Governor Horatio Sharp in 1756, the fort, left, which overlooks the Potomac River from North Mountain, provided shelter for settlers during the French and Indian Wars. During the Revolutionary War it served as a prison camp and held many Hessian troops.

141

ST. JAMES SCHOOL . . . The history of this school, six miles from Hagerstown in the Cumberland Valley, goes back to 1842, when it was opened as St. James's Hall. From 1844 until the Civil War—when it closed because the Confederates seized its head as a hostage —it was the College of St. James. In 1869 it was reopened as a secondary school. It is Episcopalian.

SPRINGFIELD . . . Stands in Washington County, on a tract named Garden of Eden by its early 18th Century patentee, Thomas Cresap—who himself was given the name "Maryland Monster" by Pennsylvanians he battled in a border dispute. The middle part of the mansion was built in 1750. Gen. Otho Holland Williams was a later occupant, and added one of the wings.

CUMBERLAND PUBLIC LIBRARY . . . This name only partly describes the historic building, for there is on its second floor an auditorium that serves the city as a civic and cultural center, too. A number of organizations meet there, and exhibitions of painting, ceramics and sculpture are held. The building dates to 1850, when it was erected as a new home for the Allegany County Academy. Then already almost half a century old, that school was the oldest in Western Maryland when it finally closed during the first quarter of this century. Its building, on Prospect Square opposite the Courthouse, became the library in 1934.

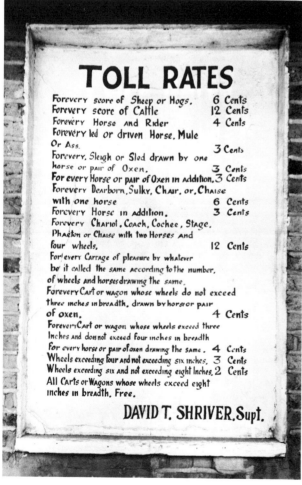

TOLL RATES

For every score of Sheep or Hogs.   6 Cents
For every score of Cattle   12 Cents
For every Horse and Rider   4 Cents
For every led or driven Horse, Mule
Or Ass.   3 Cents
For every, Sleigh or Sled drawn by one
horse or pair of Oxen,   3 Cents
For every Horse or pair of Oxen in addition, 3 Cents
For every Dearborn, Sulky, Chair, or, Chaise
with one horse   6 Cents
For every Horse in addition,   3 Cents
For every Chariot, Coach, Cochee, Stage,
Phaeton or Chaise with two Horses and
four wheels,   12 Cents
For every Carriage of pleasure by whatever
be it called the same according to the number,
of wheels and horses drawing the same,
For every Cart or wagon whose wheels do not exceed
three inches in breadth, drawn by horse or pair
of oxen,   4 Cents
For every Cart or wagon whose wheels exceed three
Inches and does not exceed four inches in breadth
for every horse or pair of oxen drawing the same, 4 Cents
Wheels exceeding four and not exceeding six inches, 3 Cents
Wheels exceeding six and not exceeding eight inches, 2 Cents
All Carts or Wagons whose wheels exceed eight
inches in breadth, Free.

DAVID T. SHRIVER, Supt.

TOLL GATE HOUSE . . . The first one placed on the old National Road, which was one of the arteries important to the growth and development of this country's resources in its early days, the building stands west of Cumberland and has been restored to this appearance. It was put up about 1833, when this part of the road was turned over to the State of Maryland by the Federal Government. Below is a chart of the tolls that were charged; it is still posted on the side of the house. The National Road ran as far as St. Louis; it is now Route 40.

HISTORIC CABIN . . . After several earlier moves, the one that was Washington's Cumberland headquarters during the French and Indian War, 1755-1758, and again in 1794 when he was commander-in-chief of the American Army, stands in that city's Riverside Park. It was restored in 1921.

AS THOUSANDS CHEER . . . On one day each spring Cumberland's airport resounds to the roar of racing sports cars and the yells of crowds as great as 65,000. Top-name drivers participate in cars fantastically expensive, many of them imported. The races aid Lions Club sight-conservation work.

DEEP CREEK LAKE . . . A year-round playground, this lake and the rolling hills embracing it offer swimming, boating, fishing and hiking in the summer, and skiing, ice fishing and ice boating in the winter. In autumn the mountain foliage explodes with color.

SKY-HIGH SWAMP . . . Atop a Garrett County ridge 2,550 feet high the 560-acre Cranesville Swamp, a public preserve, is a bit of the Far North. Because of the altitude, plants and animals characteristic of Canada and even of the true Arctic find conditions suitable here.

VIRGIN TIMBER . . . The last 40 acres of it that Maryland has left are safeguarded in Swallow Falls State Forest, nine miles north of Oakland. White pines and hemlocks, the trees tower as high as 120 feet, have trunks up to 40 inches thick, and are as old as 300 years and more.

ICE BOATING . . . This winter sport enjoyed at Deep Creek Lake when wind and ice are just right attracts "hard-water sailors" who flash by at speeds up to 50 miles per hour. In the foreground of the photograph is a snowplane that is powered by an airplane engine and propeller.

HARPERS FERRY . . . The West Virginia town made forever famous by John Brown is shown from Maryland Heights, on our side of the Potomac, with the Shenandoah River and Virginia at left. In the "bowl" just over the top of the tree in the foreground stood the arsenal Brown seized in the raid he launched from Maryland on October 16, 1859, as the start of an invasion of the South with the aim of freeing its slaves. His raid and "martyrdom" caused such national turmoil, and so sharp a cleavage between pro- and anti-slavery forces, that it has gone down in history as one of the chief contributing causes of the Civil War.

MARYLAND HEIGHTS . . . Was itself a scene of fighting when the war came. First held by Union forces, as the name on this rock there still testifies, it was taken by the Confederates in September of 1862 in an action that helped pave the way for the capture of Harpers Ferry.

HERE IS WHERE . . . Brown's raid began. It is the Washington County house—known as the old Kennedy farmhouse—in which he secretly assembled men, arms and ammunition for his attack on Harpers Ferry, about five miles away. The building has been enlarged, however, since his time.

The Civil War

MARYLAND, a State of divided sympathies a hundred years ago, has much to remember about the Civil War. In a weathered Washington County farmhouse John Brown, the Abolitionist, planned his quixotic attack on Harpers Ferry, five miles away. In February, 1861, Abraham Lincoln moved secretly through Baltimore before daybreak because a famous detective said there was a "Baltimore plot" to assassinate the President-elect on the way to his inauguration. Then on Friday, April 19— the anniversary of the Revolutionary War Battle of Lexington—Massachusetts troops were attacked by a crowd of Southern sympathizers while marching along Pratt Street from one Baltimore railroad station to another. Seventeen soldiers and civilians were killed, and many more injured. Some historians claim these were the first men killed in the war. The riot inspired James Ryder Randall to write a poem which later became the State song, "Maryland! My Maryland!" It also resulted in Federal military control of Baltimore—the city was ringed with guns pointing toward its heart—and close military supervision in much of the State. Despite this, Southern sympathy was often openly expressed, and an estimated

20,000 Marylanders took up Confederate arms (there were 62,959 Marylanders in the Union forces). There was a First Maryland Regiment, C.S.A., and a First Maryland Regiment, U.S.A., and the two fought each other at the Battle of Front Royal, Virginia.

Many raids and skirmishes were fought on Maryland soil, but there were only three important battles. The first was at South Mountain on September 14, 1862, when Union troops checked Robert E. Lee's first attempt to invade the North. Casualties amounted to about 5,000. Three days later the two armies, some 115,000 men, met a few miles to the west near Antietam Creek. This was the bloodiest one-day battle of the war.

Lee made a second attempt to invade the North in June, 1863, and when his army crossed into Pennsylvania Confederate forces ranged across Maryland from Cumberland to Pikesville. The second invasion ended in the Battle of Gettysburg. About a year later Confederate troops again marched into Maryland, this time bent on capturing Washington. In the Battle of the Monocacy, near Frederick, the Union army was beaten, but it held up the Confederates till aid reached the Capital.

CAMDEN STATION . . . It figured in two sensational events in the early months of 1861. On the night of February 22-23 Abraham Lincoln, en route to Washington to take the inaugural oath, was whisked through it secretly because of the reported plot to assassinate him in Baltimore—though whether there really was such a plot is not known to this day. Then in April came the attack on the Sixth Massachusetts Regiment as it marched from a railroad station on President Street, in near-East Baltimore, to this one on its way to protect the National Capital. Coming close on the heels of Sumter's bombardment and Lincoln's call for volunteers, this bloody riot further inflamed passions that were already high in both North and South.

TANEY HOUSE . . . In Frederick, it was the home of Roger Brooke Taney, the chief justice of the Supreme Court who wrote the Dred Scott decision, holding that Congress had no power to bar slavery from the Territories. This decision set off a pre-war storm. The desk at which Taney penned it is among his relics in the house.

WHITE'S FERRY . . . Here Gen. "Jeb" Stuart and his Confederate cavalrymen crossed back into Virginia in October, 1862, after a raid across Maryland and into Pennsylvania as far as Chambersburg. Near here, not long before, Gen. Robert E. Lee had crossed on the first invasion of the North. The ferryboat shown is today the last of many that once plied the Potomac.

FOX's GAP . . . On these smiling fields began the Battle of South Mountain, a preliminary to Antietam. Here and at several other points fighting raged September 14, 1862. The Confederates were driven back toward Sharpsburg by forces under Gen. George B. McClellan, but their stand gave Lee time to mass troops for the greater battle there a few days later.

WASHINGTON MONUMENT . . . Built by Boonsboro citizens in 1827, it was the first monument erected to honor George Washington. During the Civil War, soldiers used it as both a lookout and a signaling post. The land around it is now a State Park.

BLOODY LANE . . . At several places in the field, in the Battle of Antietam—or the Battle of Sharpsburg, as some call it—fighting was especially fierce. One such area was this sunken road, where many died, and which has ever since borne the name given here.

OLD DUNKARD CHURCH . . . Built in 1852, this church near Sharpsburg was damaged by both Union and Confederate shelling during the Battle of Antietam. A storm leveled it in 1921, but it was rebuilt in 1962 and contains many of the original bricks and timbers.

BURNSIDE BRIDGE . . . The graceful span, right, was another point of bloody combat. Gen. Ambrose E. Burnside fought his way across it—only to be driven back by the Confederates. This is one of nine stone bridges across winding Antietam Creek.

152

ANTIETAM'S RESULT . . . Although this battle lasted from dawn to dark on that terrible September 17 without a clear victory for either side, it nevertheless ended Lee's 1862 attempt to invade the North. He remained in possession of the field, which had been his initially, but his losses were so heavy that he dared not stay. The next night he retreated across the Potomac, McClellan having failed to attack again. The marker-dotted batlefield is now a National Park.

154

ANTIETAM'S COST . . . In the entire Civil War, no other single day's fighting took such a toll of brave men. Of its 50,000 troops, the Union lost more than 12,000—dead, wounded and missing. Of its 40,000, the Confederacy lost more than 9,000. The field was almost paved with bodies; along Bloody Lane they lay two to five deep. For days afterward the surrounding countryside was a huge hospital, with public buildings, stores, barns and private homes all housing the thousands of wounded. In the National Cemetery, pictured here, lie 4,773 Federal dead—many unidentified.

Monocacy . . . Striking toward Washington, 14,000 Confederate troops led by Gen. Jubal Early were given battle at this Frederick County rail junction July 9, 1864, by 6,000 Union men under Gen. Lew Wallace. Wallace was beaten, sustaining 1,600 casualties to Early's 700 in the day-long fight, but his effort gained the Capital time to bolster its defenses. Below, a reminder.

UNIQUE MEMORIAL . . . George Alfred Townsend, a correspondent for two New York newspapers—first the *Herald* and later the *World*—had this great arch erected in 1896 in honor of "Army correspondents and artists, 1861-65, whose toils cheered the camps, thrilled the fireside, educated provinces of rustics into a bright nation of readers." It stands on his former estate at Cramptons Gap, one of the South Mountain battlefields, and now is owned by the National Park Service.

POSTLUDE . . . Just as the Civil War had a Maryland prelude in John Brown's raid, it had a Maryland postlude in the assassination of Lincoln. After mortally wounding the President in Ford's Theater in Washington the night of April 14, 1865, John Wilkes Booth fled through Maryland to Virginia, where he was trapped and shot. He is buried at an unmarked spot in the Booth plot in Green Mount Cemetery in Baltimore. The cemetery, which dates from 1838, also contains the grave of Johns Hopkins.

ANTIETAM CENTENNIAL . . . In the fall of 1962 a cast of 2,200 persons from nineteen states recreated the Battle of Antietam as the highlight of Maryland's Civil War centennial observance. Cannons boomed, troops charged, and the odor of gunpowder once more was wafted across the meadows as men in blue and gray huddled behind rail fences. Briefly, the thunder and flame of yesteryear were heard and seen, then the ridges fell silent again.

ACKNOWLEDGEMENTS

MARYLAND has changed dramatically in the past decade. Her cities, suburbs and countryside echo to the vital sounds of demolition and new construction. And her people, more active and mobile than ever before, respond to the call of progress with undiminished enthusiasm.

In recording these changes, I have tried to preserve the images of Maryland's historic past, both living and symbolic, while showing the growth and expansion that typifies my State today.

Thus, this revised edition of "The Face of Maryland" is in many ways a study in contrasts; a balance between accomplishments of the last ten years, and the traditional charm and beauty of yesteryear.

In this space it has become my happy custom to thank some of the people who worked very closely with me, thus helping to bring about a logical order, after reviewing hundreds of my photographs.

First, my thanks to Stanley L. Cahn, whose tireless energy kept things moving in smooth order, and to my colleague Malcolm M. Allen for revision and writing captions that help the reader understand the meaning of the scenes.

Harold A. Williams, editor of the *Sunday Sun,* is deserving of particular thanks for his editorial assistance and seasoned judgment. Credit should also go to Hervey Brackbill whose original work on the captions form the basis of our effort.

To my patient wife Nancy these special words of thanks for the uncounted hours she has contributed to my books over the past 15 years; last of all, she snapped the picture below.

My appreciation to J. Albert Caldwell and his son Jack, who prepared the negatives and printed the book in superb Unitone, using special inks and fine dull paper.

Also to William F. Schmick, Jr.,of the *Sunpapers,* who kindly gave permission to use many of the photographs which have appeared in *The Sun Magazine,* and finally to the countless individuals who posed for my camera under trying and varied conditions.   A. A. B.

Jacket design by E. H. Hubbard, Jr.
Art direction by John F. Stubel
Lithographed by the Unitone ® Process by
    Universal Lithographers of Baltimore
Typography by Modern Linotypers, Inc. of Baltimore
Lithographed on Warren Offset Enamel Dull,
    manufactured by S. D. Warren Company
Binding by Moore & Company of Baltimore

PHOTOGRAPHING EDWARD ROSENFELD, THE BALTIMORE ARTIST

INDEX